GET RICH IN REAL ESTATE:
YOUR STEP-BY-STEP GUIDE
TO ACQUIRING PROPERTIES IN NYC

ELLIOT BOGOD

BROADWAY REALTY PUBLISHING

Get Rich in Real Estate: Your Step-by-Step Guide to Acquiring Properties in NYC by Elliot Bogod

Published by Broadway Realty Publishing, 150 Broadway, New York, NY 10038

www.BroadwayRealty.com

First Edition.

ebogod@broadwayrealty.com

ISBN: 978-1-7339484-4-9

This book and the content provided herein are simply for educational purposes and do not take the place of legal advice from your attorney. Every effort has been made to ensure that the content provided in this book is accurate and helpful for our readers at publishing time. However, this is not an exhaustive treatment of the subjects. No liability is assumed for losses or damages due to the information provided. You are responsible for your own choices, actions, and results. You should consult your attorney for your specific real estate questions and needs.

To my favorite women, with love and gratitude:

My wife Valerie

My daughter Elizabeth

My mother Alla

CONTENTS

Preface: 1

Chapter I: Foundations 3

    Rent or Own 6

    The Real Estate Buying Process 8

    The Magic Words of Real Estate 9

    The Next Hottest Trend 17

Chapter II: The City and Its Neighborhoods 20

    Battery Park City 25

    The Financial District 28

    Tribeca 37

    SoHo 41

    West Village and East Village 43

    Chelsea 47

    Midtown East 51

    Midtown West 58

    The Upper West Side 67

    The Upper East Side 74

    Harlem 78

    Washington Heights 81

    Other Boroughs in New York City 82

    Staten Island 82

    The Bronx 84

    Queens 85

    Brooklyn 88

Chapter III: Co-Ops vs Condos 91

    Definitions 91

Chapter IV: Townhouses and Brownstones..................................... **108**

Styles of Townhouses 111

The Cartier Building 115

The Four Tax Classes.. 116

Chapter V: Commercial Real Estate **123**

Office Space 123

Retail Spaces 125

Restaurants 128

Hotels 131

Garages... 136

Conversions.. 137

Own Your Business Property! 140

Leaseback... 140

Ground Leases.. 142

A Few Examples 143

Chapter VI: The Real Estate Investor Toolkit............................... **146**

Earn as you Buy, or The Secret of Success 146

The Value of Information 152

Mortgages... 156

Auctions 168

Closing Costs 171

Real Estate Taxes 173

Foreign Investors.. 175

Passive Income 179

To Sell, or Not to Sell - That is The Question.................. 182

Refinancing... 185

Depreciation.. 188

Cost Segregation... 189

1031 Exchange.. 190

Parting Ways With a Team Member.................................. 196

Chapter VII: Sell Cycles and Market Cycles **198**

The Inner Mechanics of the Market Cycle................................... 199

Why sell during a buyer's market? Why buy during a sellers' market? 204

The Mid-1990s.. 207

Turn of the Millennium 208

2002-2008 209

2008-2009 210

2009-2011 211

2011-2015 211

2015 - Present.. 212

Chapter VIII: The Investor's Team **214**

The Lawyer.. 214

The Mortgage Broker & Bank.. 216

The Title Company 217

The Appraiser.. 219

The Surveyor 220

Partners 220

Remember Your Due Diligence! 222

The Real Estate Broker... 224

Acknowledgements: 231

About the Author:... 232

PREFACE:

Thank you for picking up this book and taking your first step towards real estate success. As I guide you on this journey through the exciting world of real estate, I assume that we share certain values, including the importance of hard work and finding meaning in our daily lives and activities. If, like me, you're also passionate about being successful in business, then you will be fascinated by the endless possibilities of making money in real estate. Welcome, as we embark together on what I promise will be a fun adventure!

I have tried to make this guide informative yet concise, while also providing you with all the basic tools you will need in order to make informed choices and successful investments. I've simplified complex concepts and avoided using confusing industry talk. I believe that one of my most useful tasks here is to make difficult concepts easy to understand, remember and put into practice. In other words: easy, actionable steps with measurable results. The luxury real estate market in Manhattan is complicated enough without confusing matters more with a long, unreadable volume. Simple language is every reader's best friend.

Even though this book is short, it took me over a decade to write! In fact, having written the first draft back in 2007, I could easily have begun with one of those traditional forewords titled "What's new in the second edition". As fate would have it, the 2008 housing crisis and recession changed the rules of the game enough that the original manuscript had to be significantly upgraded.

That same year, I became a father for the first time. Fatherhood proved to be both a great responsibility and a liberating force in my life. I've always felt with deep conviction that life presents unlimited potential to those who are ready to take their destiny in hand. When you have a family to support, you suddenly find hidden reservoirs of drive and commitment. I felt that nothing could hold me back, and I was able to build a family while also building a successful and lucrative career. Real estate proved one of the rare professions where one could achieve amazing results quickly.

Upon reflection, it's probably a good thing I'm publishing this book today rather than ten years ago, as I have since learned so many industry secrets or "tricks", and deepened my knowledge of all aspects of real estate. I can't imagine advising readers or clients without the experience I've gained these past years! Now my secrets will become your secrets on your way to real estate success.

In the end it gives me great satisfaction to share what I've learned with others. I've always enjoyed guiding others and being generous with my time and knowledge. In the process I also learn new things that contribute to my life and profession. And while there's always some ego and self-interest involved in every writer's undertaking, this guide exists mainly for your benefit so that each reader will be able to achieve or surpass their real estate goals. Please feel free to reach out to me or any of my colleagues at any time with questions that you might have, and I promise to answer them to the best of my abilities.

Enough preliminaries, let's just dive in!

CHAPTER I: FOUNDATIONS

I love New York City, where I both live and work. To me, New York is unlike any other city in the world. It visits me nightly in my dreams. And even though it isn't the capital of its own state—New York—it is in fact the capital of the world.

Manhattan's architecture excites the imagination and leaves an indelible impression on anyone who's ever visited it: from the modernist magnificence of its skyscrapers, to the endless sea of cars, buses, trucks and yellow cabs, to the vast blueish expanse of the Hudson River emptying into the Atlantic Ocean. There are the sometimes deafening, thunderous groans of its underground subway cars, matched above by the constant din of people speaking in every language known to man. Here you will find every religion, nationality, culture and skin color imaginable. And that is just the beginning of what New York has to offer. The city's unsurpassed energy cannot be measured or controlled. As for the most famous of its five boroughs, Manhattan will always remain the jewel in this beautiful urban crown!

The most important topic of this book isn't New York however. In the end, it's the work itself. Yes, Manhattan is the love of my life, but it also happens to be my job. I buy and sell real estate properties there. I chose my profession a little over twenty years ago, and I love it today more than ever. I try to inject the love I feel for my great city into everything I do -whether it's purchasing an apartment or building, or completing a mortgage refinancing or sale. In turn, I hope you, the reader, will sense this love on every page and in every sentence of this book!

It sometimes seems that the old joke about every conversation in New York revolving around real estate is actually true. This isn't surprising, given how much property values continue to rise and how in-demand New York properties are! I'm convinced my passion for Manhattan and my love of all things real estate have been the main reasons for my success to date. Over the years I have been able to make very decent money selling, managing, building, and investing in Manhattan real estate, both for myself and for my clients. And now with this unique new guide at your fingertips, you can too! All you have to do is put your mind and heart into it and follow my advice and guidelines.

The book you're reading is intended as a simple guide for those who want to prosper and take pride in owning real estate in Manhattan. Making money this way is only easy, however, if you accept that the subject itself is complex by nature. If you can overcome this initial hurdle, then we can definitely make things happen for you.

I became involved in Manhattan real estate after a few years of living in New York as a young college graduate. Like many people in my position, I faced a difficult choice: to go to work for a big company and became a cog in the wheel of Corporate America, or to pursue the American spirit by going into business for myself and becoming an entrepreneur. I chose the latter… and I'm glad I did.

Being an entrepreneur or an independent business person doesn't mean that you feel free. As I've learned the hard way, being my own boss means getting up earlier than most people and working long hours: at home, in the office, even in your car driving to and from appointments and meetings. It means making hundreds of phone calls a day and scheduling and conducting dozens of meetings and conferences, showcasing properties, and solving problems for my clients and business partners. My professional life is intense and pressure-filled, but the decision to be independent turned out to be the right one for me.

Being your own boss means making mistakes, learning from them, and becoming wiser in the process. In fact, it's perhaps the best way to become a real expert in one's field. Being self-taught means I didn't have a mentor to direct and advise me and make my journey easier. In spite of the fact that my Rolodex includes some of the most renowned people in the real estate industry, I still prefer to figure things out on my own whenever possible. New solutions usually entail being more innovative and they lead to more success for everyone involved. The end result is truly satisfying: when I can sit down with colleagues and guide them through even the most convoluted concepts in real estate in a simple, easy-to-understand way, *I* become the invaluable mentor.

That's what I hope to do for you in this book. For example, I'll teach you what properties to buy in different neighborhoods of Manhattan in order to make the most money in the shortest time. Or, on the contrary, what properties you should buy and never sell but just keep for yourself.

The Manhattan real estate market is a universe unto itself, with its own unique laws and characters, ruling families, and even its own unique language. My goal in writing this book is to make that world as familiar to you as the back of your hand and help you see New York City in a different light.

The Manhattan real estate market depends on the status of the American economy as a whole, on the ebb and flow of percentage rates in sales and mortgages, on domestic and foreign politics, as well as a myriad of other factors. And yet, year in and year out, the Manhattan real estate market is the strongest real estate market in America, regardless of any outside forces and fluctuations.

Whether you own property elsewhere, or if it's your first purchase in New York, I'm assuming you are now a potential investor interested in owning a property of strategic interest that will lead you to reap the maximum economic benefits from your purchase.

Rent or Own

Here's an interesting fact: when it comes to real estate, renters far outnumber owners in Manhattan. Of all 3.2-plus million housing units in Manhattan, approximately 2.2 million are rentals. Although these are some of the most sophisticated and savvy people in the world, the vast majority of Manhattanites rent rather than own their property! 63 percent of the city's housing stock is rented, a very high number, compared to the nationwide average of 37 percent.

Having established that fact early in this book, I want to share with you my firm belief that if you want to live in Manhattan, you must - I repeat, you must! - buy and own real estate property in the city rather than rent it.

If you're currently a renter, here's my message to you: it doesn't matter how expensive owning property in Manhattan may appear to you at the first glance. You must, at any cost and as soon as possible, get out of the mass of renters and become a property owner. I don't care how hard or impossible you may think it is for you at the moment, you should still try to put together a first deposit and obtain a **mortgage** from your bank.

Every dollar of rent you pay your landlord is like throwing your money away. And I'm saying this to you even though I personally earn much of my income as a landlord!

This is just one of many paradoxes herein. Although my own livelihood depends on renters staying renters and paying me monthly, I am advising you to do just the opposite and never pay a landlord again in your life!

I want you to set your mind firmly on the goal of no longer being a renter, but on owning your home and actually investing in other properties so you can become a landlord in your own right and start receiving rent money every month. That's how your family and your kids can become more prosperous and have a much higher chance of success in the future.

I've been on both sides of this barricade. I used to be a tenant. I was foolish enough to pay monthly rent so I could live in a terrific ocean view penthouse with a huge balcony and a fireplace the size of some people's garages, in a building with a doorman and every possible service, amenity and convenience you can think of. Boy, did I love that apartment!

Looking back at that period of my life, I can tell you living in that apartment was a major mistake. I threw away a lot of money by staying there. My advice from personal hard-earned experience is the following: no matter how great your neighborhood is, no matter how attentive and caring your landlord may be, no matter how attached you are to your current apartment, if you're paying rent it's a liability that should be dropped like a hot potato. Make due haste to say farewell to it.

As a note of encouragement: if you are transitioning from being a renter to becoming a home owner, you aren't alone. In the United States, 2.1 million people bought their first home last year. Let me rephrase that: 0.84% of the entire adult population of the United States bought their *first* home last year. Almost a whole percent. The total number of homes bought the same year was 6.12 million (2.46% of the entire adult population bought new homes just last year alone). Do you think they were all multimillionaires? The median income of the first-time homebuyer is $72,000 per year. (Admittedly, you'd need a bit more per year to be able to afford property in Manhattan). 20% of first-time buyers borrowed 80% to 89% of the price of their house from a bank. 29% borrowed up to 99% (a combination of mortgage and a private loan). The median age of the first-time homebuyer is 32.

If they can become real estate investors - so can you!

According to the National Association of Realtors, 36% of all homebuyers today are millennials (37 years old or younger), and 26% belong to Generation X (38-52 years old, that's my people). The remaining 38% are buyers between 53 and 92 years of age.

I'm aware that I'm making some difficult demands on you in this book. These first steps are the hardest. The transition from being a renter to becoming a property owner is tough. It's scary because it requires a different kind of thinking compared to what you're used to. You have to leave familiar ground behind and set sail on to the open seas of ownership. The transition is difficult, costly, time-consuming and, in many ways, counterintuitive.

Allow me to quickly outline for you the recommended steps involved in the process of selecting and buying a piece of residential real estate property in New York City.

The Real Estate Buying Process

-Start by defining what kind of place you're looking to buy. Create the list of "pros" and "cons". Know exactly what kind of home you'd like to own.

-Assess your financial situation and improve it as much as possible. An apartment (and especially a house!) in New York City is not only expensive, but it requires solid financial standing that would impress building boards and banks alike. Define the price for a piece of real estate that is realistic for you, and don't disregard closing costs, real estate taxes, mortgage payments and monthly expenses.

-Explore and select possible neighborhoods. Leave no stone unturned - walk the neighborhoods on foot, study the transportation situation and local restaurants, schools and cultural venues. Read about the crime rate and any future developments in the neighborhoods that you're interested in.

-Hire an expert mortgage broker and obtain a mortgage pre-approval letter from a bank or, better yet, a mortgage commitment letter.

-Secure support from an experienced real estate broker and start looking at apartments to buy. While you're searching for the best possible place, determine who else will be included in your team.

That should include, at the very least, an expert real estate attorney, a title company, an appraiser and a surveyor.

-Once you find the right apartment, have the building and the apartment thoroughly studied by your real estate attorney. If everything is in order, make an offer, negotiate the contract -and close the deal!

I know this sounds like a lot of work and, believe me, it is. In fact, the rest of the book is dedicated to describing each of these steps in greater detail in order to give you the best tools as you embark on your journey to finding the best value in your real estate investments.

In short again, here are the five steps in a typical real estate purchase process:

1. Select a property
2. Offer is accepted
3. Sale contract is signed
4. Financing is secured
5. Closing

Once you commit to these steps, the book will work almost like magic. My job is to help you structure your real estate thinking. If you follow my guidance, you should experience success beyond what you're currently able to envision.

Speaking of magic, I have a few magic words that I will refer to moving forward. They're magical because if you understand their meaning well and integrate them into your being, they will make you think like an investor, and then your mind will force you to act like one.

The Magic Words of Real Estate

The first such magic word I'd like to introduce you to you is **equity**.

Keep that word - equity - firmly in mind. In the world of real estate (and in the bigger business universe), equity is the measure of all things and deserves the most respect.

What is equity?

Equity is *the difference between what you own and what you owe*. Structurally speaking, it's the difference in just one letter ("n" in "own" versus "e" in "owe"), but when it comes to real estate no difference is more fundamental or more profound.

Using business language, equity is the difference between the value of your assets and the value of your liabilities. Take the cost of your properties, deduct the amount you owe to your bank(s), and what remains is your equity.

From that simple explanation, you can see that if you own a valuable piece of property and owe nothing to a bank (or anybody else) for that property, then you have the maximum equity. That is the dream scenario of every investor, the Holy Grail of real estate investment. Once you're done with your mortgage, the banks will look at you with new eyes, a mass of new opportunities will present themselves to you, and it will feel to you like you've experienced a true miracle.

I've experienced that miracle and know how to help bring it about.

This book is quite simply a roadmap that will help you to find the shortest path to the miracle of maximum equity when operating in the field of Manhattan real estate. You'll learn what opportunities open up to you when you've achieved maximum equity and how to best and most quickly achieve it. You will also learn how to stop bleeding money by paying the bank's interest rate.

Later in this book we'll talk about different types of mortgages, various costs added to your mortgage when you open or close it, and fines that you may incur if you pay the mortgage too late (or too early).

Just a bit more on equity and ownership: when you don't *own* your home, but *owe* rent for it every month, you don't just have negative equity, you have *negative equity not based on any real asset*. To a bank you're not just worthless, you cost less than zero. Seen through the real estate prism as a renter, *you* are a liability to yourself. I'm being overly simplistic and dramatic here, but only a little. That's why I can't repeat it enough: you must stop being a renter. Now!

If you've chosen to invest in real estate—even outside Manhattan—then you must plan for maximum equity in your holdings.

By the way, should you happen to currently own the kind of capital that allows you to bypass the banks and mortgage altogether and pay cash for real estate properties—then I couldn't be happier for you. (I've seen cash deals in the Manhattan luxury real estate increasingly often over the last decade.) However, if like the majority of real estate investors you must take out a mortgage, I have a useful section in the book that shows you how to avoid costly mortgage-related mistakes. I'll show you how not to overpay for your mortgage, how to select the right mortgage broker who will protect your interests (yes, they do exist...), and how to get a proper and correct mortgage straight from the bank.

I'll also talk about **passive income** - another investment miracle of sorts and an equally important ingredient of your success. The common notion is that passive income is what you get paid while doing nothing. Common notions are usually wrong, and this is no exception. In reality, passive income is *what you get paid for making smart choices about how to put your property to best possible use while you own it*. You must create passive income by making those smart choices. And having passive income actually brings you special tax benefits! No matter what investment strategy you adhere to, how long you decide keep a real estate property,—or how much you've earned through the resale or refinancing of your property, you must ensure that you receive some passive income from it. Passive income is what you as an investor are paid once a month. That's your salary.

You should also have a solid grasp of another important concept: **cash flow**. Every American uses this term once in a while, but if you ask any average person what cash flow actually means, you'll get all kinds of answers, and most of them will be off-target. Even professional accountants and business people get it wrong sometimes. That's because the term "cash flow" has multiple meanings and the correct "range of meanings" has multiple components. For our purposes, we'll describe cash flow simply as *"any new money that comes your way as a result of owning real estate property"*.

Seen from that point of view, your passive income is one of your forms of cash flow. The **liquidity** of your property (*the probability of obtaining new money from selling what you own within a given time period*) is another.

I must confide that in today's complicated Manhattan real estate market your cash flow—compared to the price you pay for a real estate property—is minimal. Buying real estate at today's prices, you can't expect fast and easy cash flow. You need strategic planning and a very precise vision of how to manage the property in the most effective manner for maximum profitability and highest selling price. The cost of real estate in Manhattan can't be defined by a single word ("expensive"); it's determined by demand: the main factor dictating the prices. Any financial advisor will tell you that real estate property is not liquid, and there's no guarantee of selling any property fast or well.

But I'll tell you in all confidence and from experience that Manhattan real estate is still the most liquid and reliable in the world. This guide will show you the easiest way to sell and refinance your property, no matter how "hot" or "soft" the market becomes at any given time, and no matter how trendy (or not) a neighborhood may be. Owning real estate in Manhattan as a long-term investment will always be profitable.

Manhattan offers unique advantages to a real estate investor. Whenever possible, you should invest in condominiums. Buying a condo in Manhattan, you won't have to worry about managing the building personally. You'll be paying your common charges for that. You can diversify your real estate portfolio by buying multiple properties in different neighborhoods of the city, and benefit from the best aspects of each location. We'll discuss Manhattan's neighborhoods, as well as all the other boroughs of Greater New York City in detail in the very next chapter.

The prices for Manhattan real estate should continue to grow steadily in the course of the next few years and decades. And real estate investment comes with significant tax advantages that other types of investment simply can't match.

If you want to understand the mechanics of contemporary real estate, you need to understand the basic structure of this industry. Actually, it's not too complicated. Any real property exists on a piece of land which can be owned or rented by a person or an organization. A real estate **development** company is responsible for organizing the business process behind the real estate project. **Architects** design the property and **engineers** figure out how to build it. A **construction** company builds it. A real estate **management** company operates the property after it has been constructed. A real estate **marketing** company introduces the property to the market, and a real estate **brokerage** helps to sell or rent it.

Probably the most important thing to remember about our industry however is that real estate is not created by developers: **real estate is created by financial institutions.**

Developers are important, but it's the **investors** that make real estate a reality. We can distinguish between two "levels" of investors: major institutions that finance real estate on the massive scale and drive the creation of new properties or the conversion of the old ones - and individual investors, who typically invest in real estate properties after they've become available on the market. (Obviously, financial institutions operate with money deposited by people; they just have a lot of it, so they can afford to pay for much larger properties).

It's no secret that major corporations, banks and pension funds consider the Manhattan market to be the most dynamic and promising around. Fortunately, that market is also perfectly open to individual investors like you and me - offering investments in thousands of houses, condominiums, cooperatives, high-rise office buildings, hotels, retail spaces, and so on. It's up to every investor to decide what type of property may be the most beneficial to them. Remember: there's no single right answer. In fact, there are many right answers, depending on your goals.

Through my years of involvement in developing, selling and buying real estate, I've been able to master the sometimes subtle art of selecting the best property in the best neighborhoods of Manhattan at the best time. I will share what I've learned with you, but it will be up to you as an investor to put these principles into action. The takeaways here are useful whether you're interested in buying a home for yourself and your family, or in using real estate for profit, or even finding a business location for your company.

The next "magic word" that belongs in every intelligent investor's lexicon: **due diligence**.

Due diligence is the research, or investigation - the homework, if you will - that any self-respecting investor should do before buying a new property. Here I'd like to step back a little and say a couple of words about the fundamental conflict inherent in any real estate transaction. The obvious truth is that a buyer and a seller always pursue opposite interests. Think of this: as a buyer you want to buy the best property at the lowest price, with the most favorable financing terms for you. The seller, on the other hand, wants to sell the property at maximum profit and on the best terms. How's that for a conflict?

In any sales situation, the seller always has the advantage. The seller knows everything about the property: both good and bad - and it's in the nature of the seller to want the buyer to appreciate all the good stuff, while de-emphasizing the bad. Sometimes there's enough bad stuff to make any buyer in their right mind back out of the deal. And sometimes just one seemingly minor detail can make your life as a property owner utterly miserable and turn the piece of real estate you've purchased from an asset into a heavy burden you'll try in vain to rid yourself of for many years! (A house doesn't have to be haunted by demons to drive its owner into absolute madness.)

That's why this magic word - due diligence - must always be on your mind and on the tip of your tongue when you consider buying real estate. You must get the property thoroughly examined and study all the relevant documentation - especially the title. That exhaustive work must be done by you and your team.

Which brings us to the investor's team. This is so important that I'm giving it a full chapter in this book. You can't play the real estate game alone. The obligatory member of your team is a lawyer specializing in real estate law. Unless you pay cash for your property, your team will also necessarily include the bank. If you don't deal with the bank and/or property seller directly, you'll also need help from a mortgage broker and a real estate broker like me. You'll probably need an accountant, an insurance agent, an architect, a building contractor, and possibly a few more people. The team may vary from property to property.

I can't emphasize enough that your team is the key factor in how successful your real estate investments are going to be. The investor's team makes the difference between massive success and the ruin of even the best plans and hopes. That's why you need to collaborate with professionals—either people you know well yourself or those who have been recommended to you by your most trusted friends or partners. Work with experts who return your calls right away and whose experience and expertise you can rely on.

Back in 2004, Wharton University conducted special research on the Manhattan real estate market which concluded that apart from the size of available real estate inventory (and the corresponding demand for it), Manhattan's complex **zoning regulations** represent the most important factor affecting real estate prices. These are the laws that define, limit, and often forbid the possible uses of real estate under your ownership. Sometimes zoning regulations may negatively affect real estate prices in the entire neighborhood where you happen to own a piece of property. Adjustments and changes in zoning laws often take years and even decades to go into effect.

We'll also consider how you as an investor may be able to use your knowledge of zoning regulations in Manhattan to maximum advantage. Changes in zoning laws follow patterns and can be predicted. By correctly foreseeing a future zone change, and strategically purchasing a property in a neighborhood whose zoning laws are bound to change, you can "win the real estate lottery".

There are situations when you don't even have to wait for zoning regulations to change. You just need clear vision and the ability to recognize an immediate opportunity when you see it. You may realize that the current zoning laws allow you to raze a garage or an old industrial building and build a new hotel in their place. Or you can convert an office building into a housing complex containing multiple apartments for rent and condominiums. We'll talk about such decisions in more detail later on when we're discussing the so-called **highest and best use** - exploiting real estate property to the maximum economic advantage within a given neighborhood. Sometimes, having correctly identified the highest and best use for a property, an investor can instantly double or even triple its price. Like I said, *magic*.

Any investor operating in Manhattan (or anywhere else, for that matter) can pursue unique individual goals, have their own style of managing properties, and make the kind of profit they desire. In this book, I will show you examples of how I, and the investors I coach, aim to *double their capital every 6-12 months*. Yes, I am serious. I choose to invest only in the types of properties that deliver precisely that level of return. How is that even possible, you ask me? 100% return on investment yearly or better, when even banks only guarantee 2-3%, at most? How can I get in on that? And what's the catch?

There is a catch, of course. Isn't there always? Every investment involves risk, even the one that offers minimal return. In fact whenever you give your money to anybody, you risk never seeing that money again. Do you realize that funds in a bank account are only insured by the government up to $250,000? The rest of your money is constantly at risk, day and night... something to lose sleep over, if you're the type of person who is well off yet favors saving over investing.

What follows is an investment methodology I've been practicing and fine-tuning for many years, a plan of action that will help you to protect and grow your investment. Of course, you do need to take the first step, the leap of faith, so to speak: make the investment.

My clients always ask me: what's next? What should I expect from the Manhattan real estate market? What's the next hottest trend or transformation in the world of Manhattan properties? Which neighborhoods are the most promising today, and when is the best time to choose others?

The Next Hottest Trend

It's curious to observe how "local ripples" change over time, but longer-term "currents" remain the same. A decade ago, when I started writing this book and wrote the first version of this very paragraph, I could think of only a few neighborhoods in Manhattan that had proven themselves to be truly promising. Harlem, Chelsea and the Financial District come to mind, but I would never have dreamed in a million years of the Hudson Yards area back then. Today I can find promising, lucrative spots scattered across the entire island, and each one of them offers widely different types of opportunities.

The trend of re-zoning office and industrial neighborhoods into residential ones and converting older commercial spaces into condominiums was noticeable even twenty years ago, a decade before I embarked on this publishing endeavor.

Back in 2007 the development of "green," sustainable, eco-friendly buildings was a revolutionary new trend. Today it's a common and reasonable expectation for a building to be LEED-certified. LEED stands for "Leadership in Energy and Environmental Design," and represents one of the most popular green building certification programs used worldwide. Increasingly, new Manhattan skyscrapers include gardening, landscaping and even live trees. One of the hottest new residential developments on the Upper West Side - Waterline Square - offers organic gardens to all of its residents. Living in one of these buildings you can grow your own organic flowers and vegetables!

(You can't keep bees in the building however...at least not yet!)

A more recent and perhaps curious trend is the arrival of the so-called "slender skyscrapers" in Manhattan. Any building with the width-to-height ratio of 1/10 or less is considered "slender" from an engineering standpoint. Considering the skyrocketing land prices and relatively cheaper air rights, it should come as no surprise that some of the newest developments in Manhattan feature much more impressive width-to-height ratios: for example, 262 Fifth Avenue's 1/20 ratio or 111 West 57th street 1/24 ratio.

The most recent trend in Manhattan real estate is something that I'd refer to as the "amenities race". Developers are aggressively competing to offer the newest state-of-the-art features that provide maximum comfort, pleasure, and health to residents.

Wine storage rooms are a big attraction. Perhaps because some scientists now believe that wine prolongs life, more and more buildings offer wine storage areas. These usually include shared wine tasting areas, as well as individual lockers for personal wine collections.

Any amenity that promotes healthy living has become important. Pilates studios, yoga parlors, gyms, swimming pools, bicycle rooms - today practically every new or renovated building in

Manhattan is expected to have them. Buildings often include day spas—either building-specific or popular brands such as Setai or Miraval. Daycare centers, lounges, conference rooms, ballrooms and in-apartment garages are becoming the norm.

At the renowned 111 Murray Street, you will be offered a discount to a private jet service as an extra perk. That's probably the current winner of the "amenities race" - until the next developer includes a private opera house, a zoo, a submarine, robot personal assistants, and a fully-equipped free movie studio on premises, complete with SAG-AFTRA actors on 24/7 payroll! I'm sure my wildest imagination stops short of what they may actually come up with.

As technology progresses at an ever-increasing pace, so will the pace of offerings. Kitchen appliances, audio systems, air conditioning, and modern finishes in your apartments - everything becomes more advanced almost daily. Another trend I'm noticing involves buying properties and selling them again within 3 to 5 years so owners can keep moving to newer state-of-the-art buildings.

Back in 2007 while working on the first draft of this book, I planned to conclude this chapter with the following words:

"I'm eager to believe New York City - which began as a small Dutch colony in 1624, and now covers thirty square miles—will get a second wind and we'll soon witness a new, unprecedented blossoming of our great city."

Did someone listen to my prayers, or what?

CHAPTER II: THE CITY AND ITS NEIGHBORHOODS

Just in case you hail from out of town, I'll begin this chapter by telling you that Manhattan is one of the five boroughs that make up New York City. The other four are the Bronx, Brooklyn, Queens, and Staten Island. Odd as it may seem, even though New York City officially includes all five boroughs, people who live here often refer only to Manhattan as "the city," somehow leaving out the other four, as if they were actually in the suburbs—or in another state altogether.

Each of the five boroughs actually has its own fascinating history and unique landmarks, and each one offers plenty of opportunities for getting rich via real estate—but in this book, I'd like to focus only on Manhattan because it offers investment opportunities on a grander scale than the other four boroughs. I will also include some information about the other, so-called "outer" boroughs, just to offer some comparison and perspective, but my own personal investment preference remains Manhattan.

Manhattan is magical. Did you know there are thirty-six privately owned streets in Manhattan? Yes - you can buy a city street! A few of these private streets are famous for their beauty - for example, the gated Pomander Walk that connects West 94th and West 95th Streets between West End Avenue and Broadway, or Washington Mews in Greenwich Village. But some of them are secret venues and don't even show up on public maps!

Did you know that Manhattan has quite a number of fake buildings? For example, Mulry Square at Greenwich Avenue and 7th Avenue South - famous as the former location of a diner that inspired Edward Hopper's iconic painting "Nighthawks." It later became a parking lot and a spontaneous 9/11 memorial until a building was erected there... which is not really a building at all but a facade that disguises a giant subway ventilation shaft.

There are also at least a dozen famous haunted houses in Manhattan. These include the Morris-Jumel Mansion in Washington Heights, The Ear Inn, the romantic One if by Land, Two if by Sea restaurant and The White Horse Tavern in the West Village, as well as the Algonquin Hotel and the New Amsterdam Theater, to name just a few.

The combined square footage of all the indoor parking spaces in Manhattan equals two Central Parks.

I'd like you to take a journey with me through the neighborhoods of Manhattan and its surroundings! This will allow you to gain a solid preliminary understanding of what advantages each of the neighborhoods offers, and match these against your investment plans and expectations.

Manhattan is a dynamic, fast-paced city: always in flux, rebuilding, renovating, and discarding its old look for the sake of the new. This has been happening since it was first settled by the Dutch in the early 17th century. Every now and then, its neighborhoods acquire cool new nicknames—like "Hell's Kitchen" in Midtown, where dangerous gangs once roamed. (It's a great neighborhood now!) And once in a while an entirely new neighborhood even sprouts up—like Hudson Yards, which was built in 2012 on the old rail yards near the Hudson River between 27th Street and 34th Street. Hudson Yards, in fact, is the largest private real estate development in the history of the United States!

Younger generations of Manhattanites may not realize that not long ago a neighborhood name like "Nolita" sounded hip and new, since today it's considered a well-known place with a name that everybody recognizes. Similarly, today when I refer to the new real estate development area of 57th street as "Billionaires' Row", some of my clients may still have no idea what I'm talking about - but I'm sure that a few New York minutes from now that name will be "old news", too, and we'll have some even newer ones to get used to.

Whenever my clients are considering different neighborhoods to live or invest in, I always recommend that they gain some first-hand experience. I counsel them to spend some time in the neighborhood and walk up and down its streets at different times of the day and in the evening. I also tell them to visit both during weekdays and over the weekend, in order to soak in each neighborhood's special atmosphere. A neighborhood may look great during the week but become crowded on weekends: this may or may not bother you. My advice is that you get to know a neighborhood's landmarks and attractions on a personal level, explore its museums and restaurants, and find out as much as you can about local schools, hospitals, shops, parks, playgrounds and public transportation. You can Google the neighborhood, check out a Wikipedia article about it, or even buy a tourist guidebook. (No matter how much you already know about a neighborhood, you can usually discover something new and surprising in any one of these guidebooks!)

In the first few pages of this book I made you a bunch of promises, claiming to possess almost supernatural abilities in real estate. What I am really offering you is common sense and many years of personal experience in the field. Let me give you a little demonstration of what I mean by making a simple common-sense suggestion I wish someone had shared with me back when I was just starting out in real estate. When selecting a Manhattan neighborhood in which to buy a property, think a few years ahead and consider that neighborhood not from your current point of view, but from where you see yourself a few years in the future.

Why is that, you may ask? For two reasons.

Reason number one is really quite simple. In the course of a few years your life situation may - and probably *will* - change. If you're single today, you may find yourself in a committed relationship a few years from now (stranger things have happened), and possibly even with a couple of kids.

Reason number two: the average lifetime of property ownership in Manhattan is about five to ten years because that's the average duration of the cycle during which the value of properties appreciate. Chances are, a few years down the road you'll be selling the property you're about to buy today.

Real estate prices in New York vary greatly depending on the school district in which the property is situated. Being single with no kids today, you probably couldn't care less about the reputation of any of the local schools. Tomorrow, when you have kids, you're likely to be obsessed with the subject. And if not you, then whoever is buying your property will be.

The same goes for public transportation. Issues like the distance from the property to the nearest subway station, Path train, or bus stop are key. If you drive a car or take cabs everywhere and aren't concerned with trains or buses - think again, because in a few years you may want to sell that property, and your buyer is likely to care and pay more if it's located closer to public transportation.

If the public transportation situation in your chosen neighbor-hood isn't ideal, perhaps the word is out that it's going to improve in a few years? Is a new subway line going to finally reach your neighborhood, as the Q line recently did on the Upper East Side? Or maybe an entirely new, revolutionary form of transportation will become available, the way it happened a few years ago with Citi Bike? (Today prospective buyers, rather than asking me about subways, often enquire if there's a City Bike station nearby, something no one could have predicted even a few years ago. What's going to be next, I wonder-electric hovercraft charging pads?

Another important thing to consider is access to the neighbor-hood for lower-income workers who serve the neighborhood infrastructure. Your local hairdresser or gas station attendant may not be fortunate enough to afford a condo in your cool neighborhood, but how convenient it may be for them to get to work affects not only their quality of life, but also the price for *your* property.

Once you are familiar enough with the neighborhoods you are interested in, you should take your next steps online. Study websites such as *StreetEasy.com*, *Trulia.com*, *Zillow.com* (all three are owned by Zillow Group) or their alternative, *Realtor.com*. Visit websites that belong to such well-known real estate brokerage companies such as *Douglas Elliman* (elliman.com), *Corcoran Group* (Corcoran.com) and the new up-and-coming contender *Compass* (compass.com).

Or better yet visit *BroadwayRealty.com*, which may be the best on-line real estate site in town, (and I am not just saying this because I launched it myself!) Study the listings on that website and then call the Broadway Realty office +1 (212) 577-2270 - if you say that you discovered the number in this book, I'll help you pick the best properties for you in any neighborhood that you like.

Another curious concept you should know about is landmark preservation. In order to protect Manhattan's rich and unique architectural history, the New York City Landmark Preservation Commission selects some of its most interesting buildings as being historically valuable. Areas with a large concentration of such buildings are known as *Landmark Districts*. Such districts are governed by special real estate laws: the facades and interiors of historic buildings, for example, cannot be changed without a special permit from the Landmark Preservation Commission. If you as a property owner decide to change windows or doors in your landmark building, or simply prefer to paint its façade, you must first present your plans to the Commission, and the process of receiving the required permit may take a few months. In spite of these restrictions many Manhattan real estate investors prefer landmark districts, believing them to be the most stable and least prone to undesirable changes, due to their unique historic look and character. Such thinking is often valid, but every now and then it leads investors into a trap of sorts. If for some reason the market changes after you purchase a landmark building, you may be unable to change the building's original use or make other improvements to prevent it from becoming a loss to you financially. And sometimes modifying or restoring the façade of a landmark building involves such high expenses that the building becomes a burden for its owner, who allows it to fall into disrepair...

Let's move on and take a closer look at each one of Manhattan's wonderful neighborhoods. There is more than one way to skin a cat, and there is also more than one way to subdivide Manhattan. Some of the boundaries between neighborhoods, in fact, can seem arbitrary: like where does Nolita end and Soho begin? In spite of that, I will try to divide things up in the easiest and most practical way for readers. Purists may not like my primitive map of Manhattan neighborhoods, but I hope real estate investors will find it useful!

I propose that we begin at the southern tip of the island and move up in a sort of smooth northbound zigzag.

Battery Park City

Let's begin with Battery Park, one of the youngest neighborhoods in Manhattan. Created a little over forty years ago, the land on which the neighborhood is situated didn't even exist until its establishment. The lower part of the land was taken from the bottom of the Hudson River while the top soil itself actually existed as the ground over the current World Trade Center area). On the eve of construction for the original Twin Towers, that ground was excavated and moved in order to form the new land available for real estate development. So all the land under the foundations of Battery Park City is essentially man-made. That land itself is owned and managed by the Battery Park City Authority, a public-benefit corporation created by New York State and rented out to real estate developers and building owners under a one hundred-year contract.

I should probably mention that typically in New York City any buildings constructed on rental land are cooperatives. Battery Park City is an exception. Most of the buildings there are condominiums, with a few rentals added in for good measure. At the time of this writing, there are still fifty-five years left in the land rental contract - long enough for most banks and mortgage companies to finance condominiums in Battery Park City as if they were built on the condominium-owned land.

Real estate prices in Battery Park City are 15-20 percent lower than in most other neighborhoods of lower Manhattan, due to that rental contract. Condo owners in Battery Park City pay about 20% more for monthly services, also known as "common charges", than what they'd pay in Midtown - but this is compensated by lower prices for the condos themselves.

If less than 25 years remains under the land rental contract, the price of the residential property becomes equal to the difference between the monthly rent and the monthly service payments, multiplied by the number of months remaining in the land rental contract. Let me illustrate this with a simple example.

Let's suppose that there are 20 years (240 months) remaining on the rental contract for the land that hosts your property. The monthly service payment for your co-op or condo (including monthly tax in the case of the condo) equals $3,000 and the same apartment would be rented for $7,000 per month. The difference between the monthly rent and service cost would be $4,000. Multiply this difference by the number of months remaining on the land rental contract ($4,000 x 240), and the result - $960,000 - is the apartment price.

Often the land rental agreements include the option to renew the contract. The buyer must always calculate how the service payment will change when such contract is renewed. Most commonly, land rental agreements in New York do get renewed, even though sometimes that happens after prolonged feuds between the landowner and the renter.

Battery Park City is remarkable for its parks and its closeness to the water. It's one of my favorite neighborhoods, a "city within a city" separated from the Wall Street area by the West Side Highway. There are about 6,000 condominiums and 1,000 apartments for rent in Battery Park City. From the day they are placed on the market, a typical Battery Park city condominium or rental apartment is gone within in 4-6 weeks, given the huge demand.

In addition to being unique in its origin and type of land ownership and management, Battery Park City also features some distinctive buildings and neighborhood attractions. America's first LEED-certified residential high-rise building, *The Solaire*, is located here, at 20 River Terrace, and stands next door to another LEED-certified residential building called *Visionaire*, at 70 Little West Street. The neighborhood also features two highly prestigious hotels: the Ritz Carlton and the Conrad New York. The latter shares its address (102 North End Avenue) with the huge Regal Battery Park movie complex.

Several years ago, just around the time the United States was at the lowest point of a recession, Battery Park City received a surprise economic boost. The headquarters of Goldman Sachs, a leading global financial services firm, opened its new offices at 200 West Street. This increased the demand for residential properties, since the bankers wanted to live close to work. New restaurants sprung up seemingly overnight, including Danny Meyer's North End Grill, Shake Shack and Pier A with its Long Hall and oyster bar. Luxury retailers (such as Hermès, Burberry, Zegna, and dozens of others) all opened new locations in the Brookfield Place mall, a commercial rental conglomerate at 230 Vesey Street.

Another event that occurred in the neighborhood is the stuff of legend within the Manhattan real estate community. In 2011, a group of eleven condo buildings in Battery Park City put some pressure on the aforementioned Battery Park City Authority Corporation and managed to negotiate a deal that allowed them to lower the combined rental cost of the land by $279 million dollars. This boosted Battery Park City's residential real estate market even more. It also illustrated the fact that building owners are not powerless, even when they don't own the actual ground their buildings stand on!

Battery Park City is one of the greenest neighborhoods in the city, and it's a lot quieter than most other residential areas in Manhattan because there's practically no street traffic. Alas, there's also no subway - you'll have to walk across the West Side Highway to get to the closest train station. However, there are five Citi Bike stations here, all placed along the excellent bike lane that connects the neighborhood with the rest of the city and the Battery Park City Ferry Terminal, which offers access to the NY Waterway ferry and water taxis. The latter are becoming an increasingly regular part of many New Yorkers' commute. If you drive, you have easy and quick access to Brooklyn and Staten Island.

Living here, you'll also have the best view in the city of the 4th of July fireworks display and the yearly New York Yacht Club Regatta. As many Battery Park City apartments offer open views of the Hudson River estuary, the architects and engineers who designed the neighborhood made sure to include a lot of balconies in the floor plans. Unfortunately, the last constructed buildings here were completed in 2017, and there are no more available lots to build on in Battery Park City!

The Financial District

Our next closest destination is the Financial District, also known as FiDi - slightly to the east and just across the West Side Highway from Battery Park City. Unlike Battery Park City, the Financial District is one of the oldest neighborhoods in Manhattan - and also one of the most reputable ones. New York City's economy and the entire driving force of the city's growth started here.

More importantly, as a real estate investor you should know that at least 30% of New York City's economy - and Manhattan's real estate market - depends on what happens in the Financial District. Many of the people who purchase real estate here also work here.

The core of the Financial District is first and foremost the area bounded by Wall Street, Broad Street, Fulton Street, William Street, and of course Broadway—which cuts through the entire Financial District.

After the September 11, 2001 terror attacks, people began to distinguish between the Financial District East and Financial District West (east and west of Broadway, respectively).

There's no avoiding the subject of September 11 in any discussion of about contemporary Manhattan, especially when we talk about the Financial District. The subject defies words but has had such a profound and lasting impact on our city that I have no choice but to write about it. Every New Yorker who survived that day has been personally affected by it. In fact, I was on my way to the World Trade Center exactly at the time that the planes hit the towers, and by some amazing miracle of intuition, I decided not to go. I know people who perished in the catastrophe and several of my acquaintances lost loved ones who were in the towers when the planes hit. It was a tragedy that redefined Manhattan yet again, but we'll come back to this subject later in more detail.

Chambers Street represents the northern border of the neighborhood with Tribeca beginning north of it.

The Financial District houses AMEX, the Federal Reserve Bank, the World Trade Center, the New York Stock Exchange, and numerous office skyscrapers and residential high-rise buildings, museums, churches and synagogues, as well as the South Street Seaport and one of the most notable downtown landmarks: the Brooklyn Bridge, which will soon celebrate its 150th anniversary.

The Financial District is notable for its unusual recent history of character transformation. It used to be composed strictly of office buildings filled with hundreds of thousands of white-collar workers, bustling with frenetic activity during business hours on weekdays and emptying out almost completely every evening after six or seven o'clock. On weekends, a person walking down a street in the Financial District was a rare sight.

But over the course of the first decade of our millennium, the area has undergone a major transformation. First, the old produce market—which came with quite a smell!— moved from the Financial District to the much more suitable area of Hunts Point in the Bronx, thanks to the efforts of Mayor Rudy Giuliani.

A large number of older office buildings in the area (many of them over a hundred years old and incapable of competing in quality with new Class A office buildings of Downtown and Midtown,) have been converted into residential condominiums or apartment buildings for rent. The city government, under the leadership of Mayor Michael Bloomberg, stimulated that initiative by issuing a special 421-G tax exemption and abatement program applicable to the conversion of old commercial buildings into residential dwellings, as well as a 421-A tax exemption program targeting new developments.

The trend of converting old office buildings in the Financial District into residential properties continues today. These condos are remarkable for their large windows, huge ceilings and a level of architectural detail not available in other neighborhoods and other types of buildings. These classical features are only available in this neighborhood. Condos in such buildings are easy to sell and are in high demand among investors.

The influx of residents in the Financial District brought about the demand for resident-friendly infrastructure. Retail stores like Tiffany & Co. and Hermès opened on Wall Street. Century 21, a neighborhood landmark, opened on Church Street. Cipriani opened an ultra-luxurious restaurant, also serving as a concert and events venue, in the neoclassical building that formerly hosted the New York Merchants Exchange, the New York Stock Exchange, the United States Customs House, and the headquarters of the National City Bank. Other more recently opened restaurants in the area include *Nobu Downtown*, at 195 Broadway and *Eataly Downtown* at 4 World Trade Center.

Over the last decade, the Financial District has become even more dynamic and well-developed. More than seven hundred businesses have moved into the neighborhood since 2005, nearly 60% of them representing TAMI ("technology, advertising, media and information) and related industries. Currently the Financial District is the only area of Manhattan in which millions of square feet of commercial and residential properties are being built simultaneously! New residential buildings feature the most amazing architecture, engineering, interior designs, and amenities. Commercial buildings contain the most beautiful and technically advanced offices. As of today, residential and commercial space in the completed buildings is still being filled. Needless to say, the neighborhood continues to improve.

Don't just take my word for it. Let's look at a couple of examples - some of my favorite buildings in the area.

15 William, formerly known as The Beaver House - a 47-story condominium building, located - you guessed it - at 15 William Street, on the corner of Beaver Street, is marketed as a "vertically integrated village". These condos are equipped with fine Liebherr, Miele, and Bosch appliances. Burmese teak flooring, rainforest showers, oversized deep-soak bathtubs, adjustable louvered doors, stone kitchen counters, and so on. Imagine living in a place like that!

New York by Gehry, at 8 Spruce Street, is a spectacular 76-story apartment building designed by superstar architect Frank Gehry. The development of this building was spearheaded by Bruce Ratner, the founder of Forest City Ratner development firm, and the former city commissioner of consumer affairs famous for his fight against corruption in local commerce. The development of that building became possible because Ratner's organization was one of the recipients of federal Liberty Bonds allocated to the city to help rebuild and reinvigorate Downtown after the September 11 attacks. Even with this "cheap money", and armed with one of the best designs ever created by the great Frank Gehry, the developer ran out of funds by the time the building rose only 40 floors high and publicly announced the end of construction. Within a year and a half, new investors delivered additional funds, and the Federal Government "splurged" some more. This became possible thanks to so-called *variance* - a real estate term that refers to a special permit that includes a clause stating that the developer must allocate significant work effort toward developing public schools, squares, parks, sculptures, playgrounds, road improvements, etc., to benefit the city and the public.

In this case the first five floors of the building, decorated with dark-beige brick, were pledged to a public school. That commitment set into motion all the right political and financial levers, and the building was successfully completed. It became one of the tallest residential buildings in the world and a true gem among many of New York's most gorgeous buildings. Above the public school, the remaining 71 floors are clad in stainless steel and contain over 900 rental apartments. The building has met with universal acclaim from architectural critics, and is often compared in its beauty with such icon of Manhattan architecture as the Woolworth Building.

2016 saw the opening of *The Oculus* - an architectural complex that combines a train station, a plaza, and the largest city shopping mall in America: Westfield World Trade Center. The mall retail spaces to approximately 160 stores and restaurants -a veritable "Who's Who" of the world's most famous luxury retail brands.

The train station, officially known as The World Trade Center Transportation Hub, deserves a special mention. Ever since the Grand Central Terminal was built on East 42nd Street in 1903, downtown Manhattan has suffered from insufficient public transportation and couldn't remotely compete with Midtown until the new millennium saw the Federal government set aside a budget of two billion dollars to construct a downtown train station superior in size and capacity to the old Grand Central.

Under the power of eminent domain, also known in New York simply as "appropriation" (the right of the government to take private property for public use, on the condition of fair compensation), the Federal Government bought out a number of buildings on Fulton Street and Broadway from their owners and razed them to free the land for the transportation hub that would connect Manhattan with Kennedy Airport, New Jersey, and Staten Island. One of the world's most celebrated contemporary architects, Santiago Calatrava, designed the metal and glass building that looks as if it's hovering over the area on its huge, wide wings. The innovative design allowed the passengers waiting for the train to arrive to the underground platform to see the sky and sunlight streaming through the glass cupola. The project ended up costing twice the planned budget - four billion dollars! - making it the most expensive train station in our planet's history, and more expensive than the adjacent Freedom Tower ($3.8 billion). Regardless of its cost, the hub has achieved the goal of galvanizing Downtown and the Financial District.

Nobody would expect the Financial District to transform into the world's fashion mecca - but that's exactly what has happened, thanks to the intelligent decision made jointly by the Hearst publishing house, the Port Authority of New York and New Jersey (the developer of Freedom Tower), and The Durst Organization (the property management company). They decided to allow *Vogue* and several other fashion magazines to rent a million square feet - that's twenty floors! - in the Freedom Tower. As a result, many of the world's most prominent and influential fashion writers and editors now work in the Financial District. Needless to say, this made every fashion-minded person on the planet look at the neighborhood and take notice. These days during the biannual New York Fashion Week sponsored by Mercedes Benz, the Financial District is flooded with some of the most prominent fashion models from all over the world. These models can be seen walking around in the latest fashions and perfumes. A huge difference from the days of the old smelly produce market!

Speaking of the Freedom Tower, the observation deck on the rooftop of the tallest building in the Western hemisphere opened for business in 2015 and drew 2.3 million visitors in its first year, earning an estimated $73.6 million.

Freedom Tower is the most prominent building in the World Trade Center architectural complex, but of course it's not the only one. Buildings have also been completed at 3 WTC, 4 WTC and 7 WTC. At the time of this book's publication, 2WTC and 5WTC have yet to be built.

Next to the Freedom Tower is a monument to the tragedy that befell New York and America: *The National September 11 Memorial & Museum*. The museum collection includes more than 40,000 images, 14,000 artifacts, over 3,500 audio recordings, and more than 500 hours of video. Over 37 million people have visited the memorial since it opened in 2011, and more than 6.8 of them in 2017 alone. With its somber tone, austere minimalist design, and stated purpose of commemorating a terrifying catastrophe, the museum differs from most of the other tourist destinations in the city. But from a certain philosophical point of view, this historical monument can be seen as truly life-affirming. From here, looking at the former location of the Twin Towers replaced today with two square pools, we can reflect on our tragic impermanence in the world and embrace life.

Among other museums that draw tourists to the Financial District are such institutions as the Museum of American Finance; Fraunces Tavern a (museum and a tavern in Manhattan's oldest building, located at 54 Pearl Street -from here George Washington bid farewell to his troops during the

American Revolutionary War); the National Museum of the American Indian; the New York Police Museum; Barnum's American Museum; and the South Street Seaport Museum.

The old cobblestone streets, numerous coffee shops, bakeries and cozy little restaurants of this area remind one of old Europe with its historic and romantic feel. That's not just a coincidence; the variety of Manhattan's historic architecture is rooted in the Old World, and many of the older houses look as though they sailed one day to America over the Atlantic from England, France, or Spain along with their tenants. This may be one reason tourists from those countries frequent this area - they're drawn to something that reminds them of their home countries.

Thousands of apartments had been rented out in this area over the last few years.

Downtown is also the center of Manhattan politics and the locations of City Hall and many municipal buildings. Located mostly along Broadway, in the vicinity of Center Street and Chambers Street, these buildings are noteworthy for their uniquely beautiful architecture.

I realize throughout the previous pages I used the word "tourist" a few times. Why do I keep talking about them, and what do they have to do with Manhattan real estate?

Quite a lot actually.

First of all, you'd be surprised just how many people from outside of the United States own real estate in Manhattan. Many of them came to the country as tourists first and now they are locals, thanks to their trust in the value of New York real estate. A lot of out-of-towners come here to visit their family members currently living in Manhattan. But even guests of our city without relatives and with no plans to buy a place in Manhattan, are important to us as real estate professionals. While they're in New York, they have to stay somewhere, right? And hotels *are* real estate.

In fact, hotels are one of the hottest types of real estate in Manhattan to invest into right now. New York City is undergoing the largest hotel boom in its history. Over 18,000 new hotel rooms were created here since 2010, and 36,000 rooms are to be built in the near future! Of these, over 6,000 hotel rooms were added in Lower Manhattan (mostly in the Financial District), and 10,700 more are in the pipeline in the area.

One of the most luxurious new hotels in the Financial District is located in one of the most historically prominent buildings in the entire New York City. It's *The Beekman* - a Thompson Hotel, at 123 Nassau Street. This address is marked by the New York's first public performance of William Shakespeare's Hamlet in 1761. Yes, this theatrical masterpiece, likely completed by the Bard in 1602, had not been performed in Manhattan until nearly 150 years later. In 1883, the current, very beautiful building was completed. Back then it was known as Temple Court, and it was one of Manhattan's very first "archaic" skyscrapers. The building remained in excellent structural shape for over 130 years, and finally *The Beekman* opened here in 2016. If you want to be shocked by luxury - stop by *The Beekman* and take a peek inside. And if you want absorb it deeper, why not rent a penthouse for a couple of nights? It's only $6,500 per night.

An interesting blend of hotel and rental apartment building in the Financial District is known as an "extended stay hotel" called AKA Wall Street. Paradoxically, it's not located on Wall Street but three and a half blocks away from it, at 84 William Street. City blocks are so small here this small detail makes no difference. The project is a partnership between Korman Communities, Shorewood Real Estate Group, and Prodigy Network. It's a beautiful neoclassical building featuring 132 luxury apartments, which you can book like a hotel room. Stay indefinitely without a lease agreement, enjoy hospitality services like in a hotel, and leave at any moment! How's that for civilization? Forget fabled "southern hospitality". New York is not only the capital of money and art; today it's the capital of hospitality, too. We love our guests and want them to stay!

Perhaps more importantly than tourists, office workers, politicians, or fashion models, among the most common sights in the Financial District today are couples with baby strollers. Life truly triumphs in Downtown Manhattan!

I feel special pride for the Financial District. I opened my first office there, a small real estate bureau that included only four agents. It was located on the 8th floor of Manhattan's first skyscraper - 198 Broadway. That building has since been acquired for a very large chunk of money by the Federal Government on the basis of the above-mentioned right of eminent domain, and today it hosts the steel-and-glass entrance to the Transportation Hub. My current office is also here - just a couple of blocks down the street, at 150 Broadway. It's here that I closed most of my deals - for myself and my clients. I love this neighborhood and know almost each building and its tenants!

Here's a fun fact: the two shortest streets of New York City are in the Financial District: Edgar Street (63 feet long) and the slightly longer Mill Lane, known until 1664 as Elliot's Alley—a much better name in my opinion! Why did they have to change it?!

I could talk about my neighborhood for several chapters, but I promised to make this book short. Let's move on to a very interesting neighborhood that stretches further north and begins nearby, just across Chambers street.

Tribeca

The word "Tribeca" (originally written as TriBeCa) is an abbreviation for "triangle below Canal Street." This neighborhood was historically one of the city's most industrial, with a large number of factories and technical plants. Today it's been completely transformed and is one of the most youthful neighborhoods in Manhattan. The majority of the original industrial buildings have been fully renovated and converted into condominiums and lofts. A great number of art galleries, restaurants and schools with strong reputations have opened in the area.

Tribeca is home to the famous Tribeca Film Festival that takes place every year at the Tribeca Performance Arts Center. The purpose of that festival is to draw international attention to New York City as one of the film capitals of the world.

Celebrated actor, producer, and businessman, Robert De Niro, played a huge role in the rebirth of Tribeca. He chose Tribeca as the most promising neighborhood for his plans and almost single handedly built up a bohemian artistic community and provided comfortable infrastructure for its social networking. He opened a hotel (The Greenwich Hotel) and several restaurants (such as Nobu, Tribeca Grill, Locanda Verde and Layla) in the neighborhood. Such well-known restaurateurs as Jean Georges Vongerichten, David Bouley and Harry Cipriani followed suit.

Tribeca has a deserved reputation for its fine restaurants - other great places you should check out include *Tamarind*, *Blue Smoke*, *Pepolino*, *The Odeon*, *Tribeca's Kitchen* and *Marc Forgione*.

In the first decade of our millennium, major New York real estate developers Jack Resnick & Sons, Edward J. Minskoff, Stephen L. Green and others successfully built and sold condominium buildings in Tribeca such as 200 Chambers Street, 101 Warren Street and 250 West Street. All these buildings feature magnificent views of the Hudson and offer amenities such as gyms, garages, concierge service and a lot more. The Warren Street building hosts a Barnes and Noble, Whole Foods and Bed, Bath & Beyond.

Tribeca has seen several interesting new real estate development projects over the last few years - I'll tell you in a moment! - but its claim to fame is the abundance of lofts in old buildings, with their trademark high ceilings and open rooftop terraces. Even today, many streets here are paved with cobblestone, just like centuries ago when the neighborhood was filled with stables and horse-drawn carriages.

I consider Tribeca to be a promising neighborhood even though not every investor may be able to afford it, because it's also very expensive. It's here in Tribeca that the beautiful new 60-story new building at 56 Leonard Street set the recent real estate price record when its penthouse sold for $60 million!

Seeing these possibilities in Tribeca, developers consciously target higher and higher prices, elevating real estate to new levels of luxury. They invite world-renowned architects to work on Tribeca projects and the resulting properties are in highest demand, their prices notwithstanding. This goes both for new developments and resales/conversions.

Another stellar new building in Tribeca is the creation of celebrated developer Larry Silverstein (I'm very proud to say that he's also my former college professor). The building created such a stir that it sold out before construction even began. Depending on whom you ask, the building is known as the "Four Seasons Hotel New York Downtown" on 27 Barclay Street or "Four Seasons Private Residences" on 30 Park Place, or simply as "Thirty Park Place Building". This remarkable building is a 962-feet, 82-stories-high tower designed by Robert A. M. Stern Architects in a refreshingly conservative style. I mean this in the best way possible: it's a contemporary take on the great Manhattan Art Deco tradition! The lower half of the building is occupied by the Four Seasons Hotel - 185 rooms designed by Yabu Pushelberg, with a restaurant, bar, full-service spa and health club with pool. The upper part of the tower is filled with condominiums. Currently the penthouse costs $30 million.

Thirty Park Place is only a block away from Manhattan's unique architectural icon: Cass Gilbert's 1913 Woolworth Building - a National Historic Landmark, a New York City Landmark. Over a hundred years since its completion, it's still one of the thirty tallest buildings in Manhattan, and one of the hundred tallest buildings in America. The top part of this neo-Gothic former headquarters of the Woolworth Company was sold by the building owner Steven Witkoff to the developer Alchemy

Partners. True to their business name, the developers turned the "base metal" (office spaces) into "gold": beautiful ultra-luxury condominiums complete with stucco and gargoyles. Now you can buy an apartment in this iconic building as if you were living in an ancient fantasy castle overlooking Manhattan.

I visited a penthouse in the Woolworth Building. It's currently for sale. The asking price is $140 million. I'm curious not so much about *whether* it will ever sell - I'm convinced it will—but who the lucky buyer will be.

There's also an interesting building at 100 Barclay Street - located exactly between Tribeca and the Financial District. This Verizon-owned building is currently being converted into condominiums, and the penthouse triplex here will cost just $57 million, which is a crazy bargain by the new standards that we've discussed.

Yet another great building - also associated with Steve Witkoff, this time acting as a developer in collaboration with Fisher Brothers and New Valley - is the sixty-story, 800-foot tall 111 Murray Street, designed by KPF and the David Rockwell/David Mann team. The building began construction in August 2016 and is soon to be completed at the time of this writing (2018) - but over 80% of condos have been already sold. This building is notorious for its outrageously posh amenities - a 75-foot-long swimming pool, a 3,000 square foot private gym, a private Drybar hair salon, a bakery with a private dining room, a recreation room for teenagers, a state-of-the-art *hammam* (Turkish bath), and 20% discounts on private jet service provided by Blue Star Jets.

That level of comfort may seem absurd, unless you know the category of people most likely to live here. Tribeca is home to many celebrities: music superstars Jay-Z and Beyoncé, Taylor Swift, artist and musician Yoko Ono, actresses Meryl Streep, Gwyneth Paltrow and Claire Danes - and many others, including Robert De Niro - the "unofficial mayor of Tribeca." John Kennedy, Jr. also owned a pad in this neighborhood until his tragic demise in an airplane crash in 1999.

SoHo

There are many neighborhoods in Manhattan that may be considered young, and SoHo isn't one of them. This is one of the oldest - and most beautiful - areas in the city.

The word SoHo is an abbreviation for "South of Houston Street.". The name was coined by urban planner Chester Rapkin, and first used in his work "The South Houston Industrial Area." The name of this man, who died in 2001, is almost completely forgotten now, and yet it's Chester Rapkin's seminal urban planning work that deserves credit for saving the majority of old industrial SoHo buildings from demolition. We owe Chester Rapkin the continuous existence of some of Manhattan's most unusual architectural classics. His use of the term "SoHo" for this neighborhood was also a nod across the Atlantic, to the Old World's Soho: the artistic area in Westminster, West London, England. Nobody knows how *that* Soho was named - the official version is that "soho!" was the English hunters' cry. Who can figure out the British?

Manhattan's SoHo is unique among the city's neighborhoods for its old cast-iron buildings. These buildings can only be changed with a special permit from Landmark Preservation Commission and can never be razed. They represent great value to the city, as well as for real estate investors and developers.

It's a matter of special interest (and considerable controversy) for real estate investors that SoHo has a large number of M1 zone buildings. M1 zone buildings are regulated by the "A. I. R." ("Artist-in-Residence") law. The latter was passed in 1971 to allow for the conversion of 200 commercial lofts to residential use, on the condition that each loft contained a certified artist. The law allows a certified artist to occupy huge, thousand square-foot lofts for low rent and be confident that nobody will throw them out and deprive them and their artwork of a roof over their head.

For many years the A.I.R. law was happily ignored by literally everyone in real estate: buyers, sellers, brokers, banks and so on. The prices for SoHo lofts kept going up, and to give you the idea of what kind of "artists-in-residence" ended up occupying lofts in SoHo, I can tell you that one of them was the rock star Jon Bon Jovi, who bought his loft for a whopping $24 million.

This has changed. Over the last decade, New York's Department of Cultural Affairs became extremely strict in their approval process for artist certification. The decision is now made by two anonymous judges and their reasons for approving or rejecting each individual application remain confidential. It's currently considered close to impossible to obtain such certification. It's been reported that current residents of SoHo lofts under the "A.I.R." law have been requested to seek artist's certification, but so far the Manhattan real estate community hasn't heard of any multimillionaire evictions in SoHo due to lack of "artist-in-residence" certification.

Many real estate professionals insist that the "A.I.R." law is outdated, and there's a certain amount of aggressive lobbying for its cancellation. Today it's hard to predict in what way the situation will change, but it will.

That's why the luxury loft market in SoHo is currently on standby, so to speak. Lofts in M1 Zone buildings represent a somewhat risky investment at the moment. But what it means in the long-term is that once the situation finally comes to its logical resolution, lofts are likely to become a powerful investment. That's how it usually works: a prolonged period of "suspense" results in a market boom. If you find the idea of investing in a SoHo loft intriguing, my advice is to wait patiently and once the moment is just right take swift action.

Other than M1 zone buildings, SoHo contains many perfectly buyable, former industrial buildings that were converted in condominiums. There are also large parking lots and old garages just ready to be razed. My clients are always interested in new developments in SoHo that replace these old buildings. Demand for new development properties in this great neighborhood is simply crazy, and people are prepared to pay maximum price for them. This makes any SoHo property an expensive investment - and a smart one.

SoHo is rich with great art galleries and great stores - fashion brands like Prada, Armani, Chanel and Dior. Bloomingdales has a SoHo store as well, and so does Apple.

Let's now do a bit of "real estate hopscotch" and jump into the next two neighborhoods at once - we have a lot of ground to cover!

West Village and East Village

This area is much larger than SoHo but, in a way, quite similar. It's almost as if SoHo had been duplicated and its two main contrasting features expanded to fill a larger area just north. The West Village, an entirely historic landmark neighborhood, represents history. The East Village, on the other hand, is a developer's paradise. There are no historic limitations whatsoever there, which opens all sorts of interesting possibilities for rebuilding and new development.

As I wrote earlier in this chapter, my version of the Manhattan neighborhood map is simplified for practical purposes. I consider such neighborhoods as NoHo ("North of Houston"), Little Italy, Nolita ("North of Little Italy"), Lolita (that's actually a novel by a Russian-American author Vladimir Nabokov... I think) as parts of this larger neighborhood comprised of two halves, East and West. In all the areas I just named we see a lot of conversions and even more often, ground-up constructions.

Bond Street, one of the shortest streets in Manhattan, represents a unique opportunity for developers and architects' self-expression. Some truly unique buildings have been erected here; for example 40 Bond Street with its bright green copper façade, designed by the Swiss architectural bureau of Herzog & de Meuron. That building is quite expensive, with some record sales.

A $5 billion project named Essex Crossing is currently underway on the six or so acres surrounding the corner of Delancey and Essex streets, an area until recently occupied mostly by parking lots. This new development will bring over 1,000 new permanent jobs to the city and over 5,000 construction jobs. Once the construction is completed, it will result in 1,000 new housing units, 400,000 square feet of office spaces, 450,000 square feet of retail spaces and over 100,000 square feet of green space. This will include a public park, residential and commercial rooftop terraces, an urban farm, and publicly accessible interior gardens facing Broome Street. A bike path will connect Essex Crossing with other areas of the city. Thus, this historically run-down area will be turned into one of the most beautiful new areas of Lower Manhattan.

Greenwich Village is another "neighborhood within a neighborhood" that should be on the radar of every self-respecting real estate investor. One of the many notable new developments in this area is the Superior Ink building- a residential complex that consists of a seventeen-story condo building and nine townhouses. If you are aware of Manhattan's overall tendency to convert industrial spaces into dwellings, it should come as no surprise to learn that the complex's name is a homage to the former ink factory that used to occupy this place. Manhattan is sentimental about its history, indeed! The new buildings were designed by Robert A.M. Stern Architects and were developed by The Related Companies—another name on the tip of everyone's tongue, as this company is famous for the high quality and beauty of all their buildings.

I know the Superior Ink building fairly well - I've sold several condos in it - and I can tell you that it's not only one of the best buildings constructed in Manhattan over the last five years but one of the best investments.

Superior Ink is a bit on the expensive side, and the neighbors - like Ricky Martin—may annoy you if you're not much into celebrities. Leslie Alexander, the owner of the Houston Rockets, made a textbook real estate deal here: he bought a 6,300 square foot penthouse for $25.4 million and a week later put it up for sale for $39.1 million. He ended up selling it for $31.5 million to Mark Shuttleworth, the developer of the Ubuntu operating system and one of our planet's pioneer space tourists - who also sports a very fitting last name. So, Leslie *only* got richer by $6.1 million within a New York minute.

By the way, Mark Shuttleworth paid *$11 million less* for his 11-day space flight than for his penthouse. Just something to think about when you consider the value of Manhattan real estate. He bought the penthouse in 2011, when prices were ridiculously low by Manhattan standards. Today Mark could probably purchase a couple of round-trip tickets to Mars from Elon Musk for half the price of the same penthouse, should he put it up for sale.

Marc Jacobs, the famous fashion designer, bought one of the townhouses in the same complex. It's a gorgeous city mansion.

If you think Superior Ink is an interesting place, wait until I tell you about 150 Charles Street, developed by the Steve Witkoff of the Witkoff Group. He is one of the leading developers in NYC, with whom I have an ongoing successful professional relationship.

150 Charles Street is comparable in quality and possibly even superior to Superior Ink. There are 91 individually-designed residences in this building with over 33,000 square feet of private green space. It features flood gates as protection against any possible hurricane damage—a lesson learned from Hurricane Sandy-and an unsinkable emergency backup power generator.

Many celebrities have bought condos at 150 Charles Street, from me and my esteemed colleagues - such brokers as Leonard Steinberg and Raphael De Niro.

Jon Bon Jovi (you may remember him as SoHo's most celebrated Artist-in-Residence) bought a condo in this building for $17.25 million... and then sold it for $18.9 million. Go figure! Actor and comedian Ben Stiller bought a place there, and so did the famous New York photographer Steven Klein and supermodel Irina Sheyk, who is also a client.

Yet another seminal building in the neighborhood is 160 Leroy Street, constructed by Ian Schrager in collaboration with Herzog & de Meuron, who are known for a subtle touch of surrealism in their approach to residential architecture. Ian Schrager is a very bright and unusual star in the celestial map of New York real estate. Famous as the founder and former owner of Manhattan night clubs Studio 54 and Palladium, Schrager made an even bigger name for himself as a hotelier who revolutionized the hospitality industry by pioneering previously nonexistent concepts such as the "boutique hotel" and "urban resort." Schrager's foray into residential development is a logical continuation of his expanding sphere of influence in real estate. All his buildings are eagerly awaited and sell almost instantly. 160 Leroy Street - marketed as "possibly your last chance to own a home on the water in West Village"—has no equals among Manhattan buildings because of its curvilinear façade.

Manhattan's historic Meatpacking District deserves its own separate conversation because it changes so rapidly. Its old streets are still cobblestone-paved, and the butcher shops remain as busy as they were in the old days. Stunning new buildings go up almost daily—quicker than mushrooms after a rainy summer day—and the neighborhood has become the go-to place for retail real estate.

Companies such as Diane von Fürstenberg and Tesla opened boutiques here, and the Whitney Museum moved into a shockingly beautiful building at 99 Gansevoort Street designed by the great Renzo Piano, the winner of the 1998 Pritzker Prize and co-architect of the Centre Georges Pompidou in Paris.

In case you've never heard of Pritzker Prize before, it's the highest award in architecture, sometimes referred to as "the Nobel Prize for architects".

As for the East Village - it's a rapidly changing neighborhood that currently seems to be waiting for some kind of major transformative event that will create a new boom and define its character for decades to come. And such an event is definitely coming, based on certain signs. One such indication is the so-called "Whole Foods Market invasion." Over the years, Whole Foods has demonstrated an almost supernatural instinct for locating future real estate booms, and it is now in the East Village at 95 East Houston Street and 4 Union Square, targeting the area from two strategic angles, like two hunting velociraptors in a *Jurassic Park* movie. If that's not a sign of an impending boom, then I don't know what else could be. The market impression in the East Village is that of the "quiet before the storm", and while we wait, the general tendency is to replace anything that would qualify as a "waste of space" with financially sound, if not always artistically stellar, real estate properties.

A typical example would be a modest 10-story condo building at 24 Second Avenue on the corner of Second Avenue and East 1st Street, which replaced the East Village's last gas station. The 31 condos for sale in this building are currently on the market for anywhere between $1.125 million and $8.7 million.

Also on 2nd Avenue, a new condo building developed by Nexus Building Development Group will be constructed on the site of a 2014 gas explosion that leveled three apartment buildings.

And on that note, let's finish our review of both Villages, and take a giant leap Northwest.

Chelsea

If we had to give an award to Manhattan's most athletic neighborhood, Chelsea would win in every category, because it hosts the largest sports complex in the city: the Chelsea Piers. This complex includes three grandiose piers and a marina for mooring private boats. It also contains a huge skating rink—suitable for both figure skating and hockey—basketball courts, soccer fields, multi-story golf driving ranges, batting cages, dance studios, a wall for rock climbing, and a huge gymnastics hall.

The restaurants at Chelsea Piers include Abigail Kirsch Catering and Sunset Terrace on Pier 61.

The most famous new commercial landlord in Chelsea is none other than Google. The company's New York headquarters are located at 111 Eighth Avenue, which they purchased in 2010 for $1.77 billion. Google also announced the acquisition of a piece of property right across the street: the 1.2 million square feet of commercial space in the form of the Chelsea Market building, which they acquired from the Atlanta-based real estate investment and management company called Jamestown. The price tag? Just over $2 billion. As if that weren't enough, Google arranged to lease 250,000 square feet of commercial space at Pier 57, which extends into the Hudson River at the end of West 15th Street at 11th Avenue...and then they thought that over and asked to add 70,000 more square feet!

Google's rapid real estate expansion is significant because it shows just how important the tech sector has become for New York City's economy. Google employs 7,000 people in Manhattan. Mostly young, these typically well-educated and well-paid employees represent the new generation of possible new tenants for the prospective real estate investor interested in Chelsea—and they can be expected to grow to become real estate investors in their own right.

Many Chelsea condominiums are a short walking distance from the Piers, so living here is comparable in a way to living across the street from Central Park. The Chelsea Piers serve as "external amenities" to a number of local buildings that do not include a gym but instead offer a club membership to all tenants.

Like most of the neighborhoods in Manhattan, Chelsea has undergone considerable change over the last ten to fifteen years, transforming from mainly offices into a mostly residential neighborhood.

Chelsea is home to some mouthwatering restaurants as well. Just within Chelsey Market alone there are Atelier Robuchon, Momofuku Nishi, Gramercy Tavern, and dozens of others! It's also the location of the major art galleries: Marlboro Gallery, Gagosian Gallery, David Zwirner - and over two hundred others!

On the other hand, some of the city's poorest subsidized-living projects are also in Chelsea.

Near the turn of the millennium, a nonprofit organization called Friends of the High Line, spearheaded by neighborhood residents Joshua David and Robert Hammond and supported by multibillionaire mayor Michael Bloomberg, came up with the initiative to create a unique park out of the old elevated railway line. The park stretches from Gansevoort Street in the Meatpacking District, through Chelsea all the way up to the northern edge of the Hudson Yards on 34th Street near the Javits Center.

Once completed the park garnered massive praise and became one of the most original and beloved recreation areas for New Yorkers and tourists alike. Here you can walk among 120 types of green plants, enjoy the views of the city and the Hudson, breathe fresh air, admire artworks sponsored by the city, listen to music played by street musicians, watch theatrical performances, or sit on a wooden bench and read a book.

Along the High Line Park and all the way to 42nd street, Michael Bloomberg ordered re-zoning, and new real estate development projects sprung to life swiftly thereafter.

One of these buildings is Sky Garage - a condominium at 200 11th avenue designed by Young Woo & Associates. Nicole Kidman and her current husband, Keith Urban, bought a condo in that building, as did fashion designer Domenico Dolce, of Dolce &

Gabbana fame. Sky Garage is named after its unique "paparazzi-proof" feature. A property owner can drive their tinted-glass car into a special elevator and be lifted all the way to their apartment, equipped with an in-suite garage. A super-advanced transformable penthouse in this building, which also features two massive outdoor terraces with a 360-degree view and a secret stairway to a lower-level pad, is on the market at the reduced price of $20 million.

At 551 West 21st Street we have a storm-ready building designed by Norman Foster, the winner of 1999 Pritzker Prize. 44 condominiums on 19 floors, with prices for regular apartments ranging from $5.75 million to $17 million, and three penthouses, selling for $35+ million, the topmost penthouse has its own private rooftop swimming pool.

Another highlight of Chelsea real estate is a masterpiece residential building at 100 11th Avenue, developed by Craig Wood and Curtis Bashaw designed by the great French architect Jean Nouvel, winner of 2008 Pritzker Prize. This 23-story tower, featuring a technologically advanced "curtain wall system", is also sometimes referred to as "Vision Machine" and includes 72 residential units and such amenities as a spa, gym, and swimming pool. A semi-enclosed atrium called "The Loggia" includes fully-grown trees that appear to float in mid-air. That building - one of the best recent residential properties anywhere - went $50-plus million over budget and was completed two years behind schedule, but nobody regretted that too much because it sold exceptionally well.

Right across the street there's another modern classic: the IAC Building, developed by Georgetown Company and designed by the already mentioned Frank Gehry, sometimes referred to as the most important architect of our age. (Ghery is the winner of 1989 Pritzker Prize and a *few dozen more* top architectural awards). At 10 stories, it is short by Manhattan standards but it's been praised as one of the most attractive office buildings in the world.

As if that weren't enough, a third architectural marvel is in development alongside these two. Known as "The Eleventh" and located across the street from the IAC building at 76 11th avenue, this 800,000 square feet, two-tower mega project designed with genius-level fearlessness by Danish rebel wünderkind Bjarke Ingels and developed by HFZ Capital, is scheduled to be completed in 2019. HFZ purchased the site for this construction from Edison Properties of Manhattan Mini Storage fame for $870 million, the largest single land deal of 2015.

One of the towers will host a hotel operated by Bangkok-based Six Senses Hotels Resorts Spas and the second will be fully residential, consisting of 240 units whose prices currently begin at $4 million. Once completed, The Eleventh will be seen in all its glory from the West Side Highway and the High Line Park, and will make Chelsea even more beautiful - and a lot more profitable for real estate investors.

With that in mind, let's advance to our next neighborhood.

Midtown East

I'd like to start our journey through Midtown with Gramercy Park - a small private park in the middle of Manhattan, owned in common by the owners of thirty-nine surrounding buildings. The park is closed to the public and is always locked.

As of today, there are only 398 keys to Gramercy Park in circulation, each individually numbered and coded. 250-something of these keys are owned by individuals and the rest by buildings. These keys are difficult to come by and are even harder to duplicate. The locks are changed every year and every building pays a nominal fee of $7,500 per year for the privilege of using the park. A new key costs $350 per year and a replacement key costs $1,000 - and $2,000 for those unfortunate enough to lose the same key twice in a single year.

A key to Gramercy Park can serve as a perfect metaphor for Manhattan real estate market. It's a subtle art. Not everything about your investment in real property is tangible. Yes, you purchase a living space, but more than that you buy comfort, prestige, status, privacy - you buy *privilege*.

Invest in a condo in one of the thirty-nine buildings and you will receive that coveted key - a special selling point for these already valuable properties.

A nineteen-story building at 18 Gramercy Park South currently has a condo for sale listed for $12.5 million. The building used to belong to The Salvation Army, but prominent Manhattan property developers, the Zenkendorf brothers in partnership with Israeli billionaire Eyal Ofer and Robert A.M. Stern Architects, did a great job converting it into 16-unit residential in 2012. Every condo received a park key.

The penthouse here is owned by the omnipresent Leslie Alexander, who spent $41 million to purchase it. But you don't have to spend as much as Alexander. Right next door, 36 Gramercy Park East has a condo for sale for only $3.9 million. That's less than a four hundred thousand deposit in two installments plus a solid mortgage application-and the key is yours. The house was converted in 2010 by Mann Realty from a rent-stabilized apartment building into a 51-unit condominium. Speaking of rent, you could rent a place here for something like $6,000 to $10,000 a month-but you remember what I said before about renting? *Rent* is loosely translated (from Latin) as "throwing your money into the garbage".

Another option is 50 Gramercy Park North, a former hotel converted into condominiums by our old friend Ian Schrager, with three apartments currently listed for sale ranging from $3.95 million to $9 million. You can also rent Karl Lagerfeld's former flat here for $25,000. If you know somebody who would seriously consider such a proposition, give me a buzz and I will hook them up: I'm friends with a very compassionate psychiatrist who might be able to help with their condition!

If you prefer to enjoy Gramercy Park on a budget, I suppose you could rent a room in the Gramercy Park Hotel for slightly under $4,000-and a concierge will escort you to and from the park. He may even let you see his park key, if you ask nicely. Or you can just hop over the fence. Worked for me.

Our next destination is the nearby Flatiron district, also known as Ladies' Mile district. A bustling shopping and manufacturing area since the late 19th century, it developed over time into a place for galleries, antiques, rugs, and luxury furniture stores. Not too long ago, the district was rezoned like SoHo, from an M zone (manufacturing) to an R zone (residential). Needless to say, the area immediately became popular for conversions: former offices, factories, and warehouses were rapidly transformed into great residential properties with high ceilings and huge windows - a gold mine for real estate investors.

Just like everywhere else, the proliferation of condominiums here coincided with the influx of restaurants. The Flatiron District - and the wider Midtown East area - offers such treats for a gourmand as Eataly, Gramercy Tavern, Eleven Madison Park and Tocqueville, among many others. Yum.

If you enjoy South Asian cuisine, then you'll enjoy amazing restaurants such as Pippali, Chote Nawab, Dhaba, or Desi Galli. All of these are located in a very interesting little neighborhood informally known as "Curry Hill" - around East 27th and East 28th Streets and Lexington Avenue. Fewer people remember these days that the neighborhood used to be known as "Little Armenia" - filled with wonderful Armenian restaurants that no longer exist. The Armenian diaspora that assembled here during the first quarter of the 20th century gradually moved on, partially assimilated and scattered throughout the city and the Tri-State area. Only the old Armenian churches - Saint Illuminator's Apostolic Cathedral, the Armenian Evangelical Church, and the St. Vartan Armenian Cathedral - remain to remind us of Little Armenia and the fluidity of human life in this great city.

On to Murray Hill! Located between East 34th and East 42nd Streets, this area used to belong part and parcel to the old Murray family. The family's most prominent scion, Lindley Murray, was the world's best-selling author in the early 19th century, with titles like *"Extracts from the Writings of Diverse Eminent Men Representing the Evils of Stage Plays"* selling twenty million copies worldwide. Fittingly enough, today Murray Hill is the location of the Main Branch of New York Public Library - a National Historic Landmark building famous for its iconic lion statues symbolizing Patience and Fortitude - coincidentally, the two qualities essential for achieving success in Manhattan real estate.

Murray Hill is adjacent to the United Nations area and, hence, is well-regarded by many diplomats who choose to live here in order to be close to work. There are quite a few consulates and embassies in the neighborhood, and this mostly thanks to William Zeckendorf, Sr., a larger-than-life figure in the history of Manhattan real estate development. With the help of the Rockefeller family, it was Zeckendorf who assembled the parcel of land on which the iconic Le Corbusier-designed United Nations building rose in record time. Today some sixty years later, Arthur and William Lie Zackendorf (grandsons of the visionary mogul), in partnership with Eyal Ofer's Global Holdings, purchased a lot right across the street and built an amazing 44-story residential tower designed by Norman Foster, a famous architect greatly influenced by Le Corbusier.

Murray Hill's proximity to Grand Central Station makes it convenient for people from Long Island and Connecticut to commute to work in this area, so it's historically a popular neighborhood for people from these two areas to work in. The nearby Midtown Tunnel makes it easy for the same workers to access Manhattan by car via the Long Island Expressway.

Conversely a great number of top-paid financial industry professionals own or rent apartments in Murray Hill because they work nearby in the office buildings on 5th, Madison, Park, and Lexington Avenues. Over 250,000 people work in these buildings today. The most obvious example would be the Empire

State Building at 350 5th avenue, a 102-story art deco master-piece designed by Shreve, Lamb & Harmon, which currently hosts the offices of such companies as Walgreen, LinkedIn, and Bank of America. It's also arguably the most famous building in America, drawing nearly 3.5 million visitors every year.

Notwithstanding everything I just said, prices in Murray Hill are curiously low by today's standards, and you can often find great deals in this neighborhood.

(I hope you're taking notes!)

One of the most interesting new buildings in the area is The Langham at 400 5th avenue - a luxury, mixed-use 57-story tower of hotel rooms and residential condos. Another beauty is the 55-story 425 Fifth Avenue, a tasteful residential skyscraper, the swan song of the great postmodernist American architect Michael Graves.

A useful thing to know about Midtown East is that it's currently being re-zoned. The proposal for rezoning it has been in the works for over five years and first initiated by Michael Bloomberg, but rejected by the City Council during his tenure as Mayor. The newly-elected City Council recently unanimously approved a slightly revised proposal, passionately advocated by current mayor Bill De Blasio.

The rezoning will affect the area between East 39th Street to East 57th Street, and from 3rd to Madison Avenues, and it promises some amazing improvements. It's a process that may take some time, but we should expect in the near future that churches and historic buildings in this area will be allowed to sell their air rights. This will lead to a massive construction boom of new office buildings in the area that will revitalize the district. More stores and restaurants will also be built and, of course, this also means new residential properties will be needed in that neighborhood. Low prices will become a thing of the past, but profits will only increase.

This rezoning will have a huge positive impact on the city for another important reason: when people buy or sell any real estate in Manhattan, they usually pay taxes. A major chunk of those taxes go to the city. Just a single landowner in the area being rezoned, the famous St. Patrick's Cathedral, will have the opportunity to sell 1.1 million square feet as a result of new zoning regulations. The city expects to collect the minimum of $61.49 in tax per square foot. That's a projected $61.5 million that will help to improve the city's subway system and public spaces from a single property!

The history of New York real estate involves a jealous competition for height and beauty among developers and architects. When a new architectural miracle takes its place in the Manhattan skyline, we can't imagine any building being bigger, more revolutionary, or more beautiful. Sooner or later, inevitably, a new developer comes and boldly announces: "I have the vision and the resources to build something even better."

That's how The Trump World—a 72-story, 861-foot high tower at 845 United Nations Plaza, designed by Costas Kondylis— became the tallest all-residential building in the world in 2001, until this title was rudely snatched from it by the 21st Century Tower in Dubai. It remained the tallest all-residential building in Manhattan for almost fifteen years, however, until Harry B. Macklowe's 432 Park Avenue tower, designed by Rafael Viñoli, surpassed it in 2015 by an amazing 535 feet.

(A fun fact: at the time of this writing, the total price of condominiums sold at 432 Park Avenue had surpassed $2 billion, including the $91.1 million sale of three adjacent units to a lucky anonymous investor, to be combined into a 11,906 square feet manse, and the $87.7 sale of the top-floor penthouse to Saudi retail magnate Fawaz Al Hokair).

Then Gary Burnett came and announced Central Park Tower at 217 West 57th Street. Admittedly not part of Midtown East, and not *all-residential* (a Nordstrom department store on the first seven floors undermines its residential purity), Central Park

Tower will become the tallest residential skyscraper in the world. And it will constantly tease Midtown East residents at The Trump World *and* 432 Park Avenue buildings, by being always visible from their windows, and having its 100th floor ballroom loom high above both buildings' rooftops.

Until the next, even taller building surpasses it. There's a very good chance it will appear somewhere in Manhattan.

Let's do a quick dash through a couple of nearby neighborhoods: Kips Bay to the south of Murray Hill and Turtle Bay with its cozy little enclaves of Beekman Place and Sutton Place. I won't go into too much detail about these small neighborhoods, but I want you to remember that they represent a few blocks of prime real estate that always sell well.

A *sui generis* feature of Midtown East is the Diamond District - a single block of East 47th Street between 5th and 6th Avenues. No other street in the world has such a concentrated collection of jewelry stores in one place and people from all over the world come here to buy wedding rings and other expensive trinkets. Construction of new buildings has begun on this street with no end in sight.

Nearby, at 50 West 47th Street we have an interesting commercial building called the International Gem Tower, designed by Skidmore, Owings & Merrill, and developed by Extell with considerable tax incentives, on the condition that 80% of the building is occupied by jewelers. That's exactly how the building has been filled, and the tax incentive has been passed by the developer to the buyers of these commercial condos. One of the most interesting concepts introduced by Extell is that the ownership of property in this building allows jewelers to pass customs for their products and raw materials right in the building. Armored trucks can enter the building and go up in a powerful elevator right into the office floor. In this high-security building, staffed with armed guards, the demand for properties far exceeds the supply. Since many of my clients are in the jewelry business, I was fortunate to sell several of these office condominiums to jewelers.

No conversation about Midtown East would be complete without mentioning Rockefeller Center - a famous architectural complex that consists of 19 commercial buildings, covering 22 acres between 5th and 6th Avenues and 48th and 55th Streets. It was built on the site of the old Metropolitan Opera building during the Great Depression. During its construction between 1931 to 1939 Rockefeller Center created up to 60,000 construction jobs for the city. It gave new energy to the city and its Midtown, and helped New York recover from economic hardship in very much the same way as the construction of the new World Trade Center complex over the last few years helped New York to bounce back from the recession.

Rockefeller Center was designed by three architectural teams - Corbett, Harrison & MacMurray; Hood, Godley & Fouilhoux; and Reinhard & Hofmeister - working together as "Associated Architects". The complex is a textbook example of Art Deco, modernist architecture, a National Historic Landmark as well as a NYC Landmark. It includes Radio City Music Hall, 30 Rockefeller Plaza, International Building, British Empire Building, and La Maison Française, with the beautiful, humorously named "Channel Gardens" winding between the two latter buildings. Its lower plaza is famous for its giant Christmas tree and skating rink- a favorite recreation spot for many New Yorkers and tourists.

Let's now cross Fifth Avenue (watch out for that yellow cab! - wow, that was a close call) and explore our next neighborhood.

Midtown West

Starting from the south, Koreatown and Herald Square used to be office-only neighborhoods, but not anymore. Today there are plenty of small shops and cafés here, and I'm sure by now you can figure out why. That's right: the neighborhood became residential, and the locals have to shop and eat somewhere, don't they? Moreover, Michael Bloomberg signed the order to close several lanes for traffic and turned some of these streets into pedestrian-only thoroughfares - and when people walk the streets slowly rather than swoosh by in cars, they tend to walk into shops and buy stuff. Good for business - and for the city.

And now, for something completely different - the Garment District. It's one of the precious few Manhattan neighborhoods the city stubbornly keeps as commercial-only so that it maintains its unique character, at least for the foreseeable future.

At the end of 19th and early 20th century, and all the way into the Great Depression, the Garment District experienced a boom. It continued to be one of the most important drivers of New York's economy, and had huge impact on both the national and world economies. For example, in 1910, 70% of all women's clothes in America and 40% of all men's clothes were produced here. In order to honor this remarkable part of the city's history, it's been decided that the neighborhood must remain intact.

Madison Square Garden - a famous indoor sports and entertainment arena - is in this neighborhood. That fact is actually quite funny because Madison Square proper is a dozen blocks away on the East Side. The original Madison Square Garden used to be at 51 Madison Avenue, the current location of the picturesque New York Life Insurance Building designed by Cass Gilbert, the same guy who created the Woolworth Building in Tribeca.

Today's Madison Square Garden is home to the New York Rangers (NHL), the New York Knicks (NBA), and the New York Liberty (WNBA). According to the official chart, its seating capacity is exactly 20,789. The arena sits atop the "service door to Manhattan": Penn Station. Nowhere near as fancy as Santiago Calatrava's Transportation Hub or Grand Central, this "workhorse of public transportation" does its job, taking some 650,000 people per day to and from Manhattan. That's more people per day than the number that comes through JFK, LaGuardia, and Newark Airports combined.

I know people who refer to Penn Station as "the armpit of Manhattan" - or worse. Well, that's about to change because plans are underway to completely revamp it. At 250,000 square feet, the new Moynihan Train Hall will be larger than Grand Central and feature a dramatic translucent skylight at the height of a ten-story building. The LIRR concourses will be made nearly three times wider, and the two adjacent subway stations (on the 10th and 11th avenue lines,) will be completely rebuilt. Penn Station will have free high-quality Wi-Fi, laptop charging pads, and real-time train schedule updates displayed throughout the interior.

The project is being developed by The Related Companies, Vornado Realty, and Skanska, and supported by the Empire State Development Corporation, Amtrak, LIRR, the MTA, and Governor Andrew Cuomo. The designs were created by Skidmore, Owings & Merrill.

That's awesome news. But only a couple blocks to the west we have an even more exciting development.

An entire new residential and commercial neighborhood is being constructed and sold there - right as we speak. I'm referring to Hudson Yards - a massive redevelopment project happening on the 28-acre parcel of land between 30th and 34th Streets and 10tn and 12th Avenues.

The idea of developing *something useful* in that area has a 70-year history. Throughout the second half of the 20th century several development plans were offered to the city and promptly rejected. The most memorable of these proposals was formulated by William Zekendorf in the 1950s and Donald Trump in 1970s. The current project had been in the works over the course of the last decade and came to fruition as a result of several rounds of rezoning.

The MTA (Metropolitan Transportation Authority) owns the land and originally planned to sell it, but instead ended up offering it for lease to the best candidate in 2007. Several major developers offered their vision for the project, including such behemoths as Extell and Vornado, whose "rapper style" feud over many years is the stuff of legend within the Manhattan real estate community. In the end, The Related Companies, supported by the Oxford Properties Group, secured the 99-year lease and started developing Hudson Yards.

The project came with an interesting challenge, which Related successfully solved. A large portion of the area is occupied by John D. Caemmerer Rail Yard - a fully-operational train yard that belongs to the Long Island Rail Road, which uses the yard to store, maintain, and clean its trains in close proximity to Penn Station. To make the development possible, Related built a platform that covers the entire yard and is currently constructing the new neighborhood on top of that platform.

The cost of this cool little project is $20 billion, and it has brought 23,000 new construction jobs to the city.

Kohn Pedersen Fox Associates created the master plan for Hudson Yards, which includes 16 skyscrapers with a total capacity of over 12.7 million square feet of new office, residential, and retail space. This will include six million square feet of office space, a 750,000 square foot retail space, a cultural space, an Equinox-branded hotel, a school for 750 children, 14 acres of public open space (gardens, playgrounds, a public square and three different parks), and over 5,000 new residential units. The entire complex overlooks the Hudson River.

The first of the sixteen buildings, 10 Hudson Yards (also designed by Kohn Pedersen Fox), has been completed, and it's stunning. Coach, Inc., L'Oreal USA, European software company SAP, Boston Consulting Group, and the advertising company VaynerMedia are among the tenants.

It was recently announced that this 1.8 million-square-foot commercial building became the first commercial office building in New York to achieve the highest possible Platinum LEED rating. To earn such a rating, a building must comply with a nearly endless list of criteria. 10 Hudson Yards features gas-powered micro-turbines that generate electric power and control cold and hot water temperature in the building (twice as efficient as traditional methods,) and an innovative storm weather retention tank that collects rainwater to be used to irrigate the building's indoor landscaped terrace. Its raised flooring results in maximum-efficiency temperature control and cleaner air. The building even includes a special high-tech unit, called "Operation and Energy Control Center", which coordinates the performance of all building systems for maximum efficiency.

The next building, the residential 15 Hudson Yards, nicknamed "The Corset Tower" and designed by Diller Scofidio + Renfro in collaboration with Rockwell Group and Ismael Leyva Architects is scheduled to be completed in 2019. It will contain 285 condominiums on 71 floors, and will be integrated with the six-story cultural center known as The Shed. The Hudson Yards subway station on the 7th train line, at 34th Street and 10th Avenue connects Queens, Brooklyn and Manhattan, so now you can easily get to Hudson Yards from anywhere in the city.

I recently met with a Related Company executive who informed me that all retail and office spaces in Hudson Yards East (the first building of the development) have been 100% rented. He also said this: "Give it a little time, and people everywhere in the world will think of Hudson Yards when they think of NYC." Ambitious! - But I wouldn't be surprised.

I'd like to mention that there had been only three times throughout New York City's history when investors and developers secured ridiculously high profit margins. Each time it happened because the city needed money for building public infrastructure and gave away air rights at ultra-low prices: Hudson Yards, Grand Central - and Times Square.

I can't believe we're finally here: Times Square, the heart of the Big Apple, the tourist magnet, the home of theaters, hotels, restaurants, stores, and the seemingly endless display of billboards lighting up the night!

Nothing in the entire world is quite like it. In Times Square you can see famous Hollywood actors performing in multiple Broadway shows, day in and day out. You can greet the New Year, standing in a crowd of 200,000 people, all wearing silly eyeglasses and looking up, waiting for the ball to drop exactly at midnight on January 1, a tradition that goes all the way back to 1907 and has only been interrupted in 1942 and 1943 in observance of wartime blackouts. You can take a self-guided walking tour or participate in *The Late Show* with Stephen Colbert, *The Tonight Show* with Jimmy Fallon, or *The Daily Show* with Trevor Noah. A great attraction for kids at Times Square is National Geographic's Ocean Odyssey - not just an aquarium, but an "immersive entertainment experience".

Other nearby attractions include Madame Tussauds Wax Museum, Bowlmor bowling alley, *LOL* Times Square Comedy Club, and of course, the biggest attraction of the entire Times Square - the Naked Cowboy, a performer by the name of Robert John Burck who performs, you guessed it (almost) naked in cowboy boots and a cowboy hat!

We shouldn't forget nearby Bryant Park, with its restaurant, free summer movie screenings, and makeshift skating rink in winter.

That's all well and good, but very few people are aware of a peculiar little Times Square real estate secret: you can buy air rights here from a building owner and transfer these rights to an entirely different local building - even if that building is not adjacent to the one you bought the rights from. Don't ask me how it works. It's just what it is - the Times Square magic.

I've used the term air rights several times, but never bothered to explain what it means. It's a rather fascinating aspect of real estate. When you buy a piece of land or property, you actually acquire all the air directly above it, technically all the way to the outer limits of the atmosphere. So, buying air rights from a neighbor can allow you to build something on top of their building! And since air rights tend to be half the cost of land rights, buying air rights in Manhattan—and the resulting additional square footage that you can potentially sell or lease for even more money—has become a popular form of high-level real estate investment.

Yair Levy of Y.R. Real Estate Developers made a textbook-famous air rights deal in 2006, when he bought affordable air rights from the U.S. Postal Service and another neighboring building. By doing so, he instantly turned a 170,000 square feet parcel of land he owned on Third Avenue between 23rd and 24th street, into 300,000 square feet of real estate. He then proceeded to sell that parcel to J.D. Carlisle Development, who could then build a mixed-use residential and retail building there.

Coming up next: Hell's Kitchen, the neighborhood that stretches alongside the Hudson River from West 42nd to West 57th Street, where a real estate investor today can earn a *hell* of a lot of money. (Sorry, I couldn't resist the pun). And that's despite the fact that Hell's Kitchen is under the so-called low-density zoning ordinance, which means that a certain number of dwelling units can be built per acre of land. In tightly-packed Manhattan this limits the height of buildings at 12 stories.

This relatively low height greatly benefits areas of Manhattan located more to the East because it allows a mass of taller buildings to have beautiful views of the Hudson River and New Jersey all the way to the horizon. In return, from Hell's Kitchen you can enjoy a view of Manhattan's eastern skyline, including Times Square and Midtown.

The limit on building height may seem like a huge disadvantage, but you can rely on scrappy New Yorkers to make lemonade whenever life gives them lemons. These buildings in Hell's Kitchen often have beautiful roof decks and gardens. Very little wind blows on low roofs, so many developers take advantage of that. And guess what, you can sell a building with a rooftop garden for a lot more money than a building without one.

Another advantage is the relatively low cost of land, due to the same density restriction. A condominium built on lower-cost land in Manhattan is still a condominium in Manhattan, and any reasonable property buyers won't care that their three-bedroom condo with the view of Hudson River and the park is not on the eightieth floor. That's why developers and investors can earn very well here.

For several decades, the western and northern areas of Hell's Kitchen along and 11th Avenue were home to numerous car dealerships and repair facilities, so much that it quickly became known as Manhattan's Car District. Lately these dealerships have started leaving the area, and in some spots where zoning regulations allowed, the automobiles "yielded the right of way" to new residential buildings and hotels.

Many great new buildings are coming to western Hell's Kitchen—and a few existing ones already offer astonishing properties for sale.

Among the existing properties: Atelier (at 635 West 42nd Street, completed in 2007) - a 46-story skyscraper, developed by Moinian Group and designed by New York's master architect Costas Kondylis. Sadly, Kondylis recently passed away, leaving behind a legacy of almost ninety major New York City buildings. Atelier markets itself as "equal parts resort, art gallery, and private club" and contains 475 studios and one-, two- and three-bedroom apartments with magnificent views of Manhattan and the Hudson River. It's the tallest residential building with solar power on its roof in the United States. Amenities include concierge services; a 100-vehicle parking garage; a 12,000-square-foot health club; a rooftop lounge with terraces; free daily breakfast in the lobby; basketball and tennis court; golf driving range; movie theater; barbecue grills; free bicycles; crosstown shuttle bus, winter rooftop ice skating rink; indoor and outdoor play areas for children, in addition to weekly music classes and movie nights.

For $85 million you can buy the penthouse, which fills the entire 45th floor, and comes with such additional amenities as two Rolls-Royce Phantoms (one hardtop and one convertible); a Lamborghini Aventador Roadster; a $1,000,000 yacht with five years of docking fees paid; a vacation rental mansion at the Hamptons for the summer; a private chef and live-in butler; weekly dinner at Daniel Bouloud's Michelin-starred restaurant; the courtside seats at a Brooklyn Nets game and… two tickets to the Virgin Galactic spaceflight!

Another great example is a building called "Via 57 West", located at 625 West 57th Street. Designed with usual devil-may-care audacity by Bjarke Ingels, this residential tetrahedron is part of Mayor Bill De Blasio's Affordable Housing program. If you win a special lottery, you can get a three-bedroom here for $2,902 per month rent.

(But don't play that lottery. Even if you win, it's still three thousand bucks thrown to the gentle Hudson River breeze every month. Play a better kind of lottery instead, the one in which you win long-term: become a Manhattan real estate investor.)

Right across the street from "Via 57 Street" there's another beautiful building called The Max, which honors the memory of Max Elghanayan, the late Vice President of TF Cornerstone who was only 30 at the time of his demise. That building, designed by Arquitectonica International Corporation, is located at 606 West 57th Street. It also falls under the Affordable Housing program and the apartments are all rentals. My advice, as always, is the following: admire its beauty, but stay away. You've got bigger fish to fry.

What fish? Look up a few blocks north, and you'll see them. The most promising place to buy residential property in Manhattan today is within walking distance, and it's called Waterline Square.

And it happens to be located in the very next Manhattan neighborhood we're going to explore.

The Upper West Side

As agreed, let's begin with Waterline Square. It's an astonishing complex, comprised of three luxury towers around a public park, overlooking the Hudson with a magnificent view across the river all the way to the horizon.

The three buildings, known as Waterline Square One, Two, and Three respectively, are on sale at the same time. Even though they're positioned to form a unified architectural system, each of them is stylistically and structurally unique.

Waterline Square One is the creation of Richard Meier, the winner of 1984 Pritzker Prize. This building only offers 56 condos for sale, and they're more expensive than the other two buildings. The price of the Penthouse here is $35 million.

Waterline Square Two (designed by Kohn Pedersen Fox) is the closest to the Hudson River of the three buildings—and it's also the largest. That building currently has around 160 condos for sale. It offers the biggest variety of interior options and the lowest "common charges" or monthly fees.

Waterline Square Three—with only 47 condos for sale—is the creation of Rafael Viñoly, whom I mentioned a bit earlier in relation to his other design, 432 Park Avenue, the tallest residential skyscraper in Manhattan.

Every condo in Waterline Square features beautiful state-of-the-art kitchens and sophisticated modern appliances. There are over 100,000 square feet of indoor amenities accessible to anyone living in any of the three buildings. These include a swimming pool, a tennis court, a soccer field, a basketball court, a sound recording studio, a game room, an art studio, a gym, a bowling alley, a pet grooming spa, an indoor mini-farm, a community recreation area - as well as lunch rooms, conference rooms, and dining areas suitable for family celebrations, private conferences, and business events.

There's also a three-level residents' lounge resembling the deck of a modern luxury cruise ship designed by multi-award-winning interior architect David Rockwell, who also designed the Dolby Theater—the venue that hosts the Oscars.

In addition to indoor amenities, every building includes outdoor sitting areas and roof decks with tables and barbecue grills. Every building has a parking garage, doorman service, concierge, security, and a porte-cochère. (*Oui, c'est vrai!*)

As I said above, the three buildings surround a park with a pleasant stream flowing through it. The neighborhood hosts some amazing schools and restaurants; it's perfect for children and adults alike. In the nearby River Café, you can buy a burger or mahi tacos with beer or a glass of wine. Cipriani Food Hall is opening here in 2019—over 40,000 square feet of indoor and outdoor space.

As if that's not enough, the real estate tax for Waterline Square apartments is really low because Waterline Square is one of very few properties in NYC developed under the 20-year tax abatement program.

And, of course, the most wonderful perk of living in that section of the Upper West Side is that it has the cleanest air in Manhattan. It opens directly onto the 59th Street Promenade, where you can enjoy a quiet stroll all by yourself, with friends or with a baby stroller, all the while enjoying a great view of the Hudson— yet never feeling as if you're even in the city.

It's hard to imagine today, but all of that beautiful space used to be occupied by the West Side Rail Yards. After the bankruptcy of the Penn Central Transportation Company in 1970, Donald Trump secured the option for the land, let it lapse in 1979, and then bought the land from another developer for $115 million in 1985. By 1987, he formulated the plan to build a 152-story tower surrounded by a vast complex he originally named Television City.

Unfortunately, the plans for the super-skyscraper fell through and several city mayors had to come and go before Trump was allowed to build at least a few of the buildings he originally intended. Even that only became possible after Cary Chiang and Barbara Corcoran introduced him to a group of investors from Hong Kong and China, who bought the land but hired Trump Organization to develop it. The resulting complex of twelve buildings along the Riverside Boulevard is known as Riverside South.

Trump worked with the New York City Department of Parks and Recreation to create a beautiful green park with benches, a walking path, and a lane for bicyclists and roller skaters along the river from 59th to 72th Street. And, as a reminder of this area's railroad past, they kept a beautiful old locomotive in the park. Today it's a favorite place for local kids to play!

In 2005, the investors sold the entire project for $1.8 billion to multiple buyers. As a result, the unused portion of the land had been acquired by Carlyle Group and Extell Development Company. They, in turn, "passed the buck" to GID Development Group. And that's how Waterline Square became a reality.

To realize how architecture and engineering have been transformed over just a few decades, it's worth comparing Trump's Riverside South with the new skyscrapers being built for Waterline Square. The difference is drastic. We live in the future, it turns out.

Even though Waterline Square occupies just a small part of the land that could have been the Trump City, this development is still a massive undertaking, with a lot of "moving parts": logistical, political, and business challenges the developers needed to overcome in order to create the best-case scenario for neighborhood growth. This is usually done in exchange for something publicly beneficial the developers commit to creating, which, as you may remember from earlier pages of this book, is described using the magic word "variance."

There are some astonishing advantages to be gained in New York City's real estate by building projects that also benefit the public. For example, until very recently, every year the famous Chrysler Building used to save $18 million in tax because of its location: it stands on land that belongs to The Cooper Union for the Advancement of Science and Arts. For as many years as that private college continued to use the Chrysler Building as a recurrent example in its design studies, it could be legitimately claimed that the building was being used for "the instruction and improvement of inhabitants of the United States in practical science and art". Put another way, the Chrysler Building won $18 million every year just for being beautiful and serving as an inspiration to architecture lovers.

This changed just as I was adding finishing touches to this book! Chrysler Building was sold for $150 million dollars. Sounds like a lot of money, until I tell you that only a year ago Michael Dell, of Dell computers, bought a 10,000 square foot penthouse in One57 for a hundred million. Chrysler Building, on the other hand, is 1,195,000 square feet - and it happens to be not only one of the most beautiful symbols of Manhattan, but one of the most famous skyscrapers in the world. Now that's what I call a bargain!

My compliments to Aby Rosen, the buyer. Rumor has it, Aby plans to turn the building into a hotel, and if that's true I believe this is a brilliant decision. In the chapter dedicated to commercial real estate, I will explain to you why I think so.

But back to Waterline Square.

In this case, to ensure the smooth progression of the Waterline Square project, Extell committed to building a public school, a new junction of the West Side Highway connecting it to Riverside Drive, and to overhauling Riverside Park. In exchange they have been allowed to build over 3,000 new residences in Waterline Square and three smaller lots.

The first of these lots hosts an upscale private educational institution for boys: the Collegiate School. The second lot became One West End Tower Residences - a beautiful condominium built by Elad Group and Silverstein Properties where Morton Williams will open its supermarket later this year - a major step toward making this neighborhood even more convenient! On the third lot, 21 West End rises - a beautiful 43-story rental building from Dermot, the owner of a great number of rental buildings all over New York. This building includes commercial space on the ground floor, currently occupied by Soul Cycle and Starbucks. Dermot was also obligated by variance to build a "K-through-8" public school, designated as ES-342.

One of the greatest advantages of Waterline Square and nearby buildings is that it takes only a few minutes of brisk walking to reach Lincoln Center—a cultural hub built on 16.3 acres of land that includes the Metropolitan Opera, the New York City Ballet, the Performing Arts Library, David Geffen Hall, and the stunning Charles Revson Fountain. The city recently allocated $2 billion toward renovating Lincoln Center. This program included the renovation and expansion of the Alice Tully Hall (originally designed by renowned brutalist architect Pietro Belluschi) by the firms of Diller Scofidio + Renfro and FXFOWLE.

The Upper West Side is notable for a great number of schools for students of every age, interest, and cultural background: River School (a great preschool), Heschel School (a Jewish Yeshiva), Professional Children's School (teaching children who simultaneously pursue various artistic careers), Collegiate School, Ethical Culture Fieldston School, York Prep, and the Dwight School, all top-notch preparatory schools.

The neighborhood is also home to the New York Institute of Technology and John Jay College of Criminal Justice, to say nothing of The Juilliard School - the most famous performing arts conservatory in the world.

But the largest academic landlord in the area is Fordham University. It owns a considerable part of this neighborhood, and in 2008 it obtained permission for rezoning, allowing it to build residential properties in the area. The university immediately submitted a planning proposal, which outlined the construction of approximately 1.7 million square feet of real estate to be used for academic purposes, plus approximately 800,000 square feet of new residential real estate.

Between 2008 and 2014 they went through the first phase of development, with the intent to continue building until 2032. The construction plans for the second phase include three new buildings for graduate schools, a library, a new dormitory, a theater for university's Performing Arts program, and a huge garage.

Glenwood, one of the largest landlords and builders in the area, purchased two lots from Fordham early in the second decade of the millennium and developed two rental buildings containing approximately 600 apartments.

The neighborhood is also favored by broadcast companies. The main CBS East Coast Broadcast Center buildings is located at 524 West 57th Street, and several additional radio and TV production facilities are spread along West 57th Street, between 10th and 11th avenues. These studios transmit shows such as *60 Minutes*, *CBS Sports*, *CBS Weekend News* and *CBS Morning News*, along with many others.

The ABC Studios are even larger. Even though the main network building is on Times Square, they also have another on 66th Street, in addition to sound stages and technical facilities that occupy a huge area between Central Park and Lincoln Center. ABC's radio programs are recorded here and so is the Channel 7 News - you can see their trucks dotting the neighborhood.

CBS and ABC are two of the key employers in the neighborhood, and since broadcasting industry workers tend to be well-paid, they in turn pay handsomely for rented or owned apartments nearby.

I consider the area near Lincoln Center to be one of the most promising neighborhoods for a real estate investor because it's extremely liquid. Compared to other locations, I usually find properties here much easier to rent, sell, or buy. The majority of residential buildings in the area are rental, but there are a few condo buildings here as well.

Many massive new iconic projects were announced in the area. In 2015, Extell announced the project of a 25-story mixed-use building at 36 West 66th Street, which was to include retail space, a synagogue, and 23 floors of condos. A couple years later, the project transformed dramatically: the developer expanded the assemblage to include nearby areas. This changed the address of the new building to 50 West 66th Street.

Extell didn't stop at that, purchasing 201,000 square feet of additional air rights. This allowed the architectural firm Snøhetta to redesign the building, which will rise to become a 75-story tower. At 775 feet in height, it will be the tallest building on Upper West Side, towering some 100 feet above its nearest rival at 200 Amsterdam Avenue. That elegant mixed-use 51-story tower, developed by SJP Properties with financial backing from Midsui Fudosan and designed by Elkus Manfredi and CetraRuddy, will contain 112 residences averaging 3,000 square feet. The ground floor of this building will contain a synagogue and feature an elegant "crown" that will make it instantly recognizable.

Together, 50 West 66th Street and 200 Amsterdam Avenue promise to make a dramatic impact on Manhattan's skyline.

Let's move further north to the 70s, 80s and 90s. Real estate prices here depend on the property's proximity to the local subway line and its distance from Central Park or Riverside Park. The higher up in Manhattan you go, the fewer tourists, office workers, and even cars you will see. A lot of Manhattanites favor this neighborhood because it's quiet and you can get a good night's sleep even if your apartment is on one of the lower floors. This area is also valued for its small neighborhood stores and its many trees.

Today there are up to 5,000 townhouses in Manhattan, and most of them are located on the Upper West Side. Many investors enjoy buying apartments in these townhouses - or the entire buildings. Townhouses with stoops are valued for their grandeur and elegance.

We'll talk about townhouses more in a later chapter of this book, but to whet your appetite I'd like to briefly mention the fact that townhouse conversions are an excellent way to get rich in New York City real estate. Curious? Then keep reading!

But first, let's fly like superheroes right over and across Central Park and take a look at a very different neighborhood.

The Upper East Side

The Upper East Side could be further divided into a few smaller areas such as Yorkville, Lenox Hill, and Carnegie Hill, but for our purposes let's cover the entire area from 60th Street to 96th Street.

The Upper East Side is very different in character from Upper West Side. If the Upper West Side is cool, down-to-earth, and democratic, then the Upper East Side is posh, aristocratic, and perhaps a little too *comme il faut*. No wonder it's been called the "Silk Stocking District" by some. The Upper East Side is one of the best residential neighborhoods in Manhattan - and one of the most expensive.

You probably recall that earlier in this chapter we talked about how the proximity of public transportation increases the value of real estate in the neighborhood, even though people who are affluent enough to purchase that real estate may never even use public transportation? Well, the Upper East Side is a perfect example.

The Lexington Avenue line (trains 4, 5, and 6) have been providing easy public access to every area of this neighborhood for exactly 100 years at the time of this writing. But what boosted already high Upper East Side prices is the Second Avenue subway line, whose first phase opened just a year ago. The next phases of the project (to be completed around 2027 - 2029,) are certain to bring further price increases.

The new subway line will have a positive impact on public access to the neighborhood. To begin with, it will decrease crowds on the Lexington line. This will make the old line more comfortable and reduce the average travel time through the Upper East Side by 10 minutes—precious time to busy New Yorkers! And furthermore, the new subway line can make you rich. How is that, you may ask? Investors purchasing real estate property on Upper East Side will benefit from the additional massive increase in its value due to the completion of this subway line. This is an obvious example of how you can use easily available information to predict above-average growth in real estate prices, invest smart, and make good money.

The Upper East Side is notable for its high concentration of Manhattan hospitals: Lenox Hill Hospital, Cornell University Medical Center at New York Presbyterian Hospital, Memorial Sloan Kettering, and Mount Sinai Hospital, to name just a few. There are also over forty reputable public and private schools here, as well as Hunter College - one of the best colleges within the CUNY (City University of New York) system.

Of course, we have to mention Museum Mile, which stretches along Fifth Avenue from 82nd Street to 110th Street and is actually three blocks longer than a mile. Starting with the Metropolitan Museum of Art at 82nd Street, the remarkable list of museums includes The Neue Galerie of German and Austrian Art (86th Street), The Solomon R. Guggenheim Museum (88th Street), The National Academy Museum and School of Fine Arts (89th Street), The Smithsonian Institution's Cooper-Hewitt, the

National Design Museum (91st Street), The Jewish Museum (92nd Street), The Museum of the City of New York (103rd Street), El Museo del Barrio (105th Street), and The Museum for African Art (110th Street).

And that's just Museum Mile. The Upper East Side also includes such important cultural institutions as The Frick Collection, Asia Society, 92nd Street Y, The Colony Club, Goethe Institute, The Irish Georgian Society, The Society of Illustrators - and such important art galleries as Acquavella, Kraushaar Galleries, Katharina Rich Perlow Gallery, Salon 94 and Anita Shapolsky Gallery.

Considering the fact that the Metropolitan Museum of Art's collection alone could be tentatively valued at over half a trillion dollars, it's hard to assess the total worth of all the artworks consolidated in this relatively small acreage. So, if you're looking for a nice additional niche to invest in parallel to your investments in Manhattan real estate - invest in a Rembrandt. The prices for art and real estate will probably go up at about the same rate.

Like Midtown East, the Upper West Side hosts a tight concentration of embassies, diplomatic missions and consulates - and it also contains quite a few expensive residential buildings. Most of them are all-rentals or cooperatives. Good luck getting approved by a co-op board on the Upper East Side! We'll discuss the co-ops vs. condominiums (non-)dilemma later in this book. I can tell you some horror stories about co-ops that will make your blood curdle.

Anything west of Lexington Avenue all the way to Fifth Avenue is the most expensive prime real estate in Manhattan. The townhouse market serves as an excellent example. A single-family Upper West Side townhouse that costs $5-$10 million, will easily cost twice as much on the Upper East Side.

Traditionally the Upper East Side was "reluctant" to admit new developments, but the situation has changed over the last couple of years. It's not remotely as dynamic as on the Upper West Side.

Major development companies like Extell and Related are setting things in motion for the Upper East Side. New developments such as 520 Park Avenue, The Clare, The Easton, The Kent and 180 East 88th Street are among some twenty or so condominium and rental buildings currently being constructed in the neighborhood and marketed to wealthy young renters and buyers.

Roosevelt Island, although not technically in Manhattan, is also an interesting place to consider, though relatively few people are conscious of the fact that real estate prices on Roosevelt Island are much lower than those in Manhattan. And Roosevelt Island is a quick and easy ride from Manhattan by car, bus, or funicular.

Most of the residential properties on Roosevelt Island are rentals, and all of them offer great views of Manhattan, with monthly rent lower than in Manhattan.

During Michael Bloomberg's mayoralty back in 2011, Jacobs Technion-Cornell Institute—a joint venture between Cornell University and the Israel Institute of Technology—won the bid for real estate development of Roosevelt Island, offering to build a Cornell Tech campus on the island. They broke ground in 2015, and the first building opened in 2017, offering premises for 30 professors and 300 students. This is an important project for our city that will create 28,000 jobs, including 8,000 academic jobs, and will result in the creation of 600 new business, $23 billion in economic activity over a 35-year period, and an additional $1.4 billion in taxes. By the completion of the project the Cornell Tech campus will occupy 12 acres of land. Students from 62 countries will study there in beautiful modern buildings with great views of New York City.

We've almost reached the end of our journey, with only a few neighborhoods left to review.

Harlem

Like most other big Manhattan neighborhoods, Harlem can be further divided into smaller parts. East Harlem, also known as Spanish Harlem, stretches east from Fifth Avenue, up from East 96th Street to slightly past East 138th Street and all the way to the Harlem River in the north. Central Harlem is bounded on the south by Central Park North and stretches between Fifth Avenue and Frederick Douglass Boulevard all the way up to 155th Street. Finally, there's West Harlem, whose border zigzags around the Columbia University campus roughly between 110th and West 125th Street, West 155th Street to the north, and Riverside Park and the East River the West. We could even divide these areas further, into smaller areas like Manhattanville, Hamilton Heights, Sugar Hill, and so on, but for our purposes, all of this constitutes Harlem.

Named after the Dutch city of Haarlem, this neighborhood has experienced several historic "demographic waves." Originally occupied by the Native American tribes called the *Manhattans* and the *Lenapi*, it became home to several small German and Dutch settlements in the early 17th century. During the American Revolution, the British burned it to the ground. By the late 19th century the neighborhood became predominantly Jewish and Italian, with a gradual influx of Puerto-Ricans and African-Americans until the 1930s when the neighborhood was about 70% black.

Throughout its history, Harlem's population struggled with poverty. It's also been home to important trends, especially those related to African-American culture. The period from 1918 to the mid-1930s saw the birth of the Harlem Renaissance - an explosion of intellectual and creative activity among black musicians, artists, playwrights and actors that had a massive impact on culture all over the world. Harlem-born styles over the years have influenced fashion, dancing, and such wide-ranging musical genres as jazz and hip-hop.

Probably the most famous Harlem landmark is the neoclassical Apollo Theater, located at 253 West 125th Street and designed by George Keister. The building was renovated in 2005. Other landmarks include the neo-Gothic/neo-Tudor Abyssinian Baptist Church (at 132 West 138th Street); the brutalist Adam Clayton Powell Jr. State Office Building (designed by Ifill Johnson Hanchard to resemble an African mask); the neo-Romanesque James Bailey's House (10- St. Nicholas Place at West 150th Street); the Italian Renaissance-themed Graham Court (developed by William Waldorf Astor and designed by Clinton and Russell during late 19th century Harlem real estate boom); the 13-story Hotel Teresa (famous for its terracotta façade designed by Edward and George Blum and completed in 1912) - and dozens of others.

Harlem is also location of several landmark districts. Mount Morris Park Historic District, for example, and Manhattan Avenue, the West 120th-123rd Streets Historic District and the West 147th-149th Streets Historic District. This neighborhood is truly a world of its own, worthy of being explored, loved, and respected.

Harlem also has more churches and religious organizations than any other Manhattan neighborhood. This fact is important for any person who is serious about real estate, because religious organizations own a lot of land in Manhattan, and they are also the most likely sell both land and air rights. This happens due to the decline in church attendance, forcing religious institutions to sell their land, as well as the many beautiful buildings they own. These historic buildings are often suitable for residential conversion and transformation into office spaces.

Harlem is easily reachable by public transportation. All the trains that traverse the Upper West Side and Upper East Side (numbers 1 through 6 and letters A through D) go to Harlem. Theoretically, this should have made Harlem a more expensive neighborhood. However, Harlem has been home to people who were priced out of other areas of Manhattan, and the neighborhood is filled with public housing projects that aren't going anywhere in the foreseeable future. Real estate developers are aware of that fact, and that's why you'll notice that most of the newer buildings constructed are rentals rather than condominiums.

Having said that, Harlem started undergoing rapid change in recent decades. Of all Manhattan neighborhoods, Harlem is the most prone to gentrification. Harlem also offers a very attractive 25-year tax abatement to developers—the longest such abatement in all of Manhattan. Year after year we see small private houses being razed and modern apartment buildings constructed in their place.

For example, the recently completed metal-and-glass, semicircular 11-story building "Circa Central Park" (at 285 West 110th Street) features 38 terraced residences designed by FXCollaborative. It hugs the North-East sector of Frederick Douglass Circle and features apartments that each offer their owners a gorgeous view of Central Park. Most of this building has sold fast and well, but it still has several condominiums available.

Another notable recent development is 11 Central Park North. This beautiful 19-story building developed by Athena Group and designed by Hillier Architects and SCLE Architects provides a view of the park and Midtown Manhattan behind it to everyone who lives here. In 2008, penthouses in this building sold for $8 to $12 million; Harlem had never seen these kinds of prices before.

Recently, the City Council approved the rezoning of East Harlem. This represents interesting news for Manhattan real estate because it will bring nearly 4,000 new residential units into the neighborhood and add $25 million to improving the famous outdoor market: *La Marqueta*. It will also allocate $83 million to improving the Harlem River Greenway Link between West 125th and 132nd streets and a $15 million investment to the East River Esplanade. It will also pour $50 million into public housing in the area and add 1,288 affordable units to the neighborhood's private development sites.

This inevitably brings our discussion to the one of the richest and most prestigious landlords in Upper Manhattan: Columbia University. The price of education at Columbia is one of the highest in the United States, and yet, notwithstanding its price, a diploma from this Ivy League institution is coveted by students and their parents because it opens doors and opportunities for graduates like no other college in New York. That's why Columbia University's budget continues to grow, becoming similar to that of a small country. The growing university needs more campus space and more real estate, expanding its reach throughout the Upper West Side, West Harlem, and as far north as Washington Heights.

Two years ago, Columbia University obtained a rezoning permit to build several thousand new apartments. The university's current expansion budget is $7 billion. They plan to build nearly 1,000 university residential units, plus new laboratories on 2.6 million square feet, in addition to 296,000 square feet of utility space, on 17 acres of land. With this massive undertaking, the university has also committed to spending $150 million on community benefit projects. This will create 1,200 constructions jobs per year for 22 years, 6,399 permanents jobs, and $2 billion per year of estimated economic activity. This should lead to a massive transformation of West Harlem.

And finally, we've reached our northernmost neighborhood.

Washington Heights

If we want to be picky, we could talk about Washington Heights, Hudson Heights, Fort George and Inwood separately - but let's agree that for us, Washington Heights means "everything that's in Manhattan to the north of Harlem".

It's a big neighborhood located on highland and unlikely to ever be flooded. In fact, Bennett Park in Washington Heights is officially known as the highest natural point of Manhattan.

The area is unbelievably beautiful and quiet, with a large number of old churches and cemeteries, as well as old tenement buildings. There are also several beautiful parks. Its greatest cultural attraction - the Cloisters Museum - was built in the middle of Fort Tryon Park. Yeshiva University is a major property owner here: it owns a big campus and a lot of adjacent land. New York Presbyterian Hospital and Columbia University also own a considerable share of the area.

Being far from Downtown and Midtown, Washington Heights is relatively inexpensive compared to all other areas of Manhattan. Here you can find good deals on property - to rent and buy. Recently Washington Heights saw a few new developments, and more are coming soon. The rezoning of Manhattan's northern-most area of Inwood is the latest news, and promises to add 1,300 new permanently affordable apartments.

Other Boroughs in New York City

Staten Island

Originally named "Staaten Eylandt" in 1609 by none other than Henry Hudson, this is the third largest (58.5 square miles) and least populated (about 479.5 thousand people) borough of New York City. It is sometimes lovingly referred to as "the forgotten borough" by its own inhabitants, and not too spoiled by excessive attention from the city's government. Staten Island became a part of New York City in 1898, but nearly seceded from the city again a century later—in fact 65% of State islanders voted for secession during a recent public referendum in 1993—but the attempt was ruthlessly blocked in the New York State Assembly. The island was once notorious for being the home of the world's largest man-made structure, which coincidentally also happened to be the world's largest trash heap: the Fresh Kills Landfill. Currently that landfill is being converted into a 2,200-acre park.

Staten Island is big on parks: it includes thousands of acres of state parks and forests, as well as privately owned woods.

The population is diverse, and notable for its large Italian and growing Russian communities. It also has the largest Sri Lankan population in the world outside of the island of Sri Lanka itself.

Staten Island has the lowest crime rate in the city.

Some notable attractions include the Staten Island Zoo, Historic Richmond Town, the Jacques Marchais Museum of Tibetan Art, the Staten Island Botanical Garden, The New York Chinese Scholar's Garden and the National Lighthouse Museum, among others. And of course, let's not forget the free Staten Island Ferry, which connects Staten Island with Manhattan for both locals and tourists.

Until recently Staten Island maintained the reputation of having little to offer in terms of real estate - just a bunch of small houses owned by lower-middle-class families. That status is about to change. As a professional who has seen poor neighborhoods transformed into new hot beds of real estate activity, I can tell something interesting is going to happen to Staten Island within the next decade.

Nearly $1.6 billion is currently being allocated by the city and various public and private organizations toward making Staten Island a better place to live. Empire Outlets, a huge outlet center, is opening on Staten Island this year. The mall will include over 100 stores, such as Nordstrom, Columbia Sportswear, as well as Shake Shack and a hotel. The New York Wheel - the world's second largest Ferris wheel, is planned to open to the public in 2019.

Prices make Staten Island attractive. Here, about an hour away from the overpriced Manhattan, you can still buy a single-family house for $200,000.

For you, as real estate investor, this is a great opportunity for generating passive income. You can purchase three or four houses in Staten Island for the price of a single studio condominium in Manhattan and lease them to tenants. In the longer term, this means that once the prices in Staten Island start going up—and they will—you will be able to sell your properties at a significant profit.

Let's take a superhero jump from here, fly over the water, bypass Manhattan, and land slightly to north of the island, in the next unique borough.

The Bronx

The Bronx may have gotten a bit of a bad rap among real estate investors, due to its checkered track record of public safety. It is true that its 15th Congressional District, located at the southern-most area, is known as one of the five poorest (and most criminally troubled) residential areas of the entire United States (!), but The Bronx, like any other borough of New York City, is extremely diverse. It includes such affluent neighborhoods as Riverdale, Fieldston, Pelham Bay, Pelham Gardens, City Island and Country Club, among others.

The borough is named after its founder, 17th century Swedish settler Jonas Bronck, and is the only borough of New York City to have the distinction of including the definitive article "the" before its name! The Bronx is the only borough of the city located on the mainland. At 42 square miles and with a population just over 1.4 million, it's the second smallest borough of the city in both size and population.

Known as "the cradle of hip-hop" and the home of New York Yankees, the borough is notable for such great attractions as The Bronx Zoo, The New York Botanical Garden, The Bronx Academy of Art and Dance, The Bronx Museum of Arts, The City Island Historical Society and Nautical Museum, and perhaps its most unusual cultural tribute, the Lorelei Fountain and the Heinrich Heine Memorial, created by sculptor Ernst Gustav Herter.

Formerly the outcast among the five boroughs, the Bronx is currently undergoing what is already been labeled as "the new wave of gentrification" by more skeptical observers, and as "the Bronx Revival" by more positively-minded people. Even the South Bronx - the neighborhood that until recently was the least likely to attract the attention of any level-headed real estate investor - is on the radar for its real estate promise. It's even being referred to by the recently coined, somewhat facetious moniker SoBro. Currently this area, as well as many others, is being reinvented as an area for multiple new affordable housing complexes—all rentals.

As for the opportunities of today that may be of interest to a real estate investor, I'd like to mention the seemingly modest but financially promising Skyview Riverdale at 5700 Arlington Avenue. Quite a way farther north, it almost borders the city of Yonkers. It's a sprawling 23-acre complex, comprised of three 20-story towers. A former co-op, it's been renovated and converted into one- to four-bedroom condominiums by Myles J. Horne and ABC Properties. Even though it's not remarkable for its architecture, the complex offers attractive amenities such as a private Olympic size outdoor pool with a children's splash pool and surrounding lido deck, a large park, basketball and tennis courts, a health club, and onsite full-service restaurant and catering service. All available at a much low cost compared to Manhattan prices, a one-bedroom here costs $304,000 and a four bedroom, $742,000. To investors looking for passive income opportunities, Skyview Riverdale offers something to consider.

Now let's now hop east and take a quick look at -

Queens

Largest in size (178 square miles!) and second largest in population (with over 2.3 million people living in it), Queens was named after the former Portuguese Princess Catherine of Braganza, Queen Consort of England, Scotland, and Ireland and the wife of King Charles II. A fun fact that resonates well with my own immigrant background: almost half the current residents of the borough of Queens weren't born in the United States!

Queens has its own recognizable vibe: cheerful, busy, streetwise, hopeful. Queens is officially recognized as having the third most diverse population among all counties in the entire United States, and the most diverse population in New York State, mixing people of Chinese, Puerto-Rican, Russian, German, Korean, Salvadoran, African, Bosnian, Indian, Italian, Irish, Greek, Vietnamese, Mexican, Nepali, Pacific Islands origin - and countless others! 138 languages are spoken in Queens!

The borough offers plenty to explore: a branch of the Museum of Modern Art, the Museum of the Moving Image, the Noguchi Museum, the Queens Botanical Garden, the New York Hall of Science, Citi Field (the home of the New York Mets) and Arthur Ashe Stadium (the home of US Open Tennis Championship). It's also the location of both major New York Airports—JFK and LaGuardia - and the place where the best concert grand piano in the world, Steinway & Sons, is still being handcrafted today, like 160 years ago.

Such notable American cultural icons as the photographer Robert Mapplethorpe, singer Paul Simon, filmmaker Francis Ford Coppola and the punk rock band The Ramones all hail from Queens... and so does the controversial press-hating, social media-loving real estate developer—turned US President, Mr. Donald Trump.

To segue nicely back to the subject of real estate, the borough of Queens is undergoing a major residential boom these days, on the scale larger than anything happening in Brooklyn or the Bronx - with the westernmost area of the borough, Long Island City, being the epicenter of this trend. The closeness to Manhattan and relatively lower prices make Queens interesting to the thousands of people looking to buy their first property. At the time of this writing, a whooping estimated 40,000 new residential units are being built in Queens, and it's predicted by experts that the speed of growth of the inventory will only continue to increase!

In addition to residential properties, notable is the growth of the hotel industry in Queens: the number of hotels in Long Island City alone has grown from 8 to 30 in the past decade.

Areas such as Jamaica and the Rockaways are also growing fast.

I'd like to mention one curious new development project here, although strictly speaking, it doesn't represent a direct investment opportunity. The project I'm speaking about is ALTA LIC. Even though most of the 30 floors in that building, located at 29-22 Northern Boulevard in Long Island City, are filled with 467 rental units, 13 more floors of floors, operated by Ollie, offer the "all-inclusive co-living platform" - a set of shared two- and three-bedroom suites, with such amenities as an outdoor movie theater, an indoor swimming pool, a co-working space, a rooftop lawn, and a pet spa.

As for real estate investment opportunities proper, the one I'm watching is Galerie, at 2218 Jackson Avenue, just across the street from Queens's branch of MoMA. Designed by ODA New York, and developed by Adam America Real Estate and Vanke US, with interiors by Paris Forino Design, Galerie offers 183 condos ranging from studios to three-bedroom units, and in prices from $595,000 to over $2.5 million. The 13,000 square feet of amenities include a permanent curated art gallery, port cochère and 24/7 attended lobby, a landscaped courtyard featuring an Allen Glatter sculpture, a lounge, a party room, a library/workroom, a fitness center with an indoor pool, a pet spa and a landscaped roof deck.

Astoria holds a special place in my heart. It's here that I rented my very first apartment where I came to New York some thirty years ago...

And finally, the last borough of New York City for us to take a look at, before we move on to our next chapter is:

Brooklyn

I love Brooklyn. I lived and worked there for a while when I was a kid, ran businesses there and honed my entrepreneurial mind here in Brooklyn's green and not-so-green streets. My mother lives there today and I visit her as often as I can with my wife and kids, and we have amazing family dinners and gatherings in her house at least once a week. On weekends, we drive to Brooklyn to spend time with her, and also to practice tennis at our favorite Brooklyn gym, MatchPoint.

I'm sure you gathered from the earlier part of this chapter that the borough of Manhattan is pretty diverse. Well, the same can be said about Brooklyn, but on a much larger scale! Manhattan's fame and appeal may disguise the fact that Brooklyn is about five times larger (it occupies almost 97 square miles, compared to Manhattan's slightly under 23).

That's a lot of space for real estate, and believe me that space is being used!

Brooklyn is the second largest borough in New York City - and the most populated, with nearly 2.7 million people residing in it. It's ironic that the borough is named after the tiny Dutch town of Breukelen, population 14.6 thousand, over three times smaller than that of Sea Gate, the smallest neighborhood in *our* Brooklyn?

There are thousands of great things to experience in Brooklyn. These include the famous Coney Island amusement park, Brooklyn Academy of Music, the Brooklyn Art Museum (New York's largest museum in sheer physical size, at 560,000 square feet and containing 1.5 million artworks, the second largest public art collection in the United States), the Brooklyn Children's Museum, the Soldiers' and Sailors' Arch at the Grand

Army Plaza and the adjacent Prospect Park, the Brooklyn Botanic Garden, Barclay's Center (the home of the Brooklyn Nets and New York Islanders), Jamaica Bay Wildlife Refuge, Coney Island Amusement Park, and the New York Aquarium.

Brooklyn is home to a number of distinct ethnic and religious communities: Jewish, Chinese, Caribbean, African-American, Latino, Russian, Ukrainian, Polish, Italian, Muslim, Irish, Greek, Korean and many others. Each community maintains and develops its own unique culture - and cuisine!

Brooklyn is becoming increasingly more luxurious, with many neighborhoods as convenient and culturally advanced as those in Manhattan - and almost as expensive. Remember when I mentioned that Whole Foods Markets is the greatest predictor of what neighborhoods to invest in next? Guess what, Whole Foods is already in Brooklyn.

Brooklyn is famous for its historic brownstones, some of them truly unique and at least as beautiful as those in Manhattan. If you're considering investing in a townhouse, Brooklyn offers terrific, though only marginally more affordable, alternatives to Manhattan.

You can also buy a single, two-family or multifamily house in Brooklyn. New or old, the choice is massive and you can purchase them at a fraction of the cost of some of the luxury penthouses in Manhattan. This means you can potentially develop a sizable portfolio of multiple real properties in Brooklyn and use them for generating passive income.

Of course, there are new developments that may be of interest to you as a prospective investor. Among them, probably the most notable one is The Greenpoint, located in the eponymous neighborhood of Brooklyn, at 21 India Street. It's a 40-story residential building designed by Ismael Leyva Architects and marketed by City Habitats New Developments. In accordance with the new standard of mixing different types of properties in the same building, The Greenpoint offers 368 rental units as well as 95 condos. Should you decide to invest in a property here, your purchase will come with the 25-year tax abatement, and the amenities will include private port cochère, 24-hour attended lobby, waterfront terrace and lounge, a co-working space, a billiards room and children's playroom, a basketball court, parking space, outdoor courtyard, a sun deck and a few other niceties.

Element88, at 88 Withers Street, developed by Rybak and BK Developers and designed with a certain degree of panache and bold nonchalance by Zproekt Artchitects, is a new 9-story building containing 33 one-, two-, and three-bedroom condos. The building offers a 6,000 square feet park and recreation area on its second floor, complete with walkways and park benches. Fitness center, private workspaces, a game room and a wine cellar complete the picture.

Quay Tower, at 50 Bridge Park Drive, might be the most promising (and most expensive) new development, and proof that the view means a lot in real estate. Most of the two- to five-bedroom condos in that building will have permanently protected views of the East River and Manhattan Skyline—which explains why prices for two-bedroom units start at $1.9 million. The amenities include a state-of-the-art 2,500 square foot fitness center, children's room, bicycle storage room, music room, pet wash, Amazon Smart Home integration and The Sunset Lounge, which features the most incredible view of Manhattan one might ever hope for.

CHAPTER III: CO-OPS VS CONDOS

Let me ask you this: how is New York City different from all the other cities in America?

In million different ways, I'm sure, but when it comes to real estate, one notable characteristic of Manhattan may come as a surprise to you: it's the predominance of cooperative housing over condos. In Chicago, for example, there are an equal number of cooperatives and condominiums, but in Manhattan cooperatives currently represent 70% of *all owned and sold residential properties.*

It's also useful to remember that 51% of *all* Manhattan apartments are *rentals,* and only 41% are owner-occupied. The remaining 8% are vacant or seasonal. Many of the renters will eventually become owners (especially if they listen to my persistent advice) and, at some point, will face the question of whether they should choose a co-op or a condo as their preferred form of ownership.

So what's better: a co-op or a condo?

I have a very straightforward answer to that question, but first I want to show you the steps that led me to that answer.

For starters, it helps to know the difference between the two.

Condominiums and cooperatives represent two different approaches to the problem of *shared ownership.* This should make sense to you as investor because when we discuss residential real estate in Manhattan, most often we're talking about buildings that contain multiple units, sold separately.

Definitions

When you buy a **co-op**, you do not become an owner of any real estate property. Instead, you purchase the percentage of shares of the corporation that owns the building and the land, as well as all the rights, including the air rights.

On the other hand, when you buy a **condo**, you become the owner of an individual unit of a real estate property, as well as (and it's very important to understand) *a co-owner* of a shared common area of that building. That is why it's called *con-dominium*, which means "co-ownership" in Latin.

And that's all there is to it!

Well, almost. There are also "condops" and "sponsored apartments - but we'll get to them a bit later. Of course, there are also single-family dwellings, such as townhouses, which you can own in their entirety without sharing anything with anybody.

Cooperative housing has existed in Manhattan since the last quarter of the 19th century. In an article from November 1882 titled "The Problem of Living in New York," *Harper Magazine* described several co-ops and mentioned plans to build more. Most of the co-ops in Manhattan, as well as New York's other four boroughs, owe their existence to the Urban Homesteading Assistance Board. The Urban Homesteading Assistance Board is a nonprofit organization that in 1974 began to advocate for the conversion of over 1,600 foreclosed rental buildings into co-ops, and over the subsequent decade and a half greatly grew in their clout. Their influence brought about the famous 1980's co-op boom in New York City when it seemed that the greatest ambition of every real estate developer in the city was to discover a rental building yet-untouched by co-op fever and convert it.

As of today, Manhattan has approximately 95,000 condominiums. And if you do some easy math based on the percentage I mentioned a few paragraphs above, you'll be able to deduce that the number of Manhattan co-ops roughly equals 190,000 and the total number of all owned and sold residential units of both types in New York City is about 285,000.

Today, the market emphasizes condos, which makes for some interesting statistics. Thirty years ago, from 1987 - 1989, Manhattan saw 461 conversions of buildings from rentals to co-ops, which again constitutes 70% of all co-op conversions since that time till today. New co-ops, developed over the last few years, can be counted on the fingers of one hand.

I'd like to share a couple of curious examples of these recent co-ops.

My favorite is 100 Barrow Street, a beautiful new development building by the Toll Brothers. Designed by Barry Rice Architects in the conservative, "buttoned up", neo-Flemish style, the building, situated on the corner of Barrow and Greenwich Streets in West Village, includes 33 residences designed by Brooklyn-based Bernheimer Architecture. The apartments feature custom bathroom and kitchen fixtures designed and fabricated by Watermark Design. The amenities include a wine cellar, a residents' lounge, a fitness center with a sauna and steam room, a pantry and large kitchen, a children's playroom, a bike room and a pet spa.

A very different kind of example is a The Mark Hotel and Co-Op, which is rich in character and tradition. This is not a new development but a conversion from a hotel to a mixed-use building, which in addition to a hotel now includes a small number of co-op residences. Originally known simply as "The Mark Hotel", this spectacular building was designed in the Renaissance Revival style by Simon I. Schwartz and Arthur Gross and completed in 1927.

I hope you will forgive me a brief digression, but these two architects deserve a special mention here. Working between the late 1890s and the end of Great Depression, they designed a number of apartment buildings in Morningside Heights north of West 96th Street. But the two are more famous for being the architects of the "Ghostbusters Building" at 55 Central Park West and *notorious* for designing The Majestic at 215 West 75th Street, a building with hidden stairways and secret doorways which used to host a bordello that brought writers, actors, mobsters, and politicians together during the "roaring 20s".

Their building, The Mark, located at 25 East 77th Street on the corner of Madison Avenue, was purchased by Alexico Group in 2006 with the stated purpose of completely renovating it and making a partial conversion to a co-op. In 2009, superstar designer Jacques Grange created bold new interiors for The Mark, combining classic design with extreme modernity. Working on that project, Jacques Grange supervised several famous creative sub-contractors, such as Ron Arad, Eric Schmitt, Paul Mathieu, Mattia Bonetti, and Vladamir Kagan.

As a mixed-use building, The Mark includes 100 hotel rooms and 56 ultra-luxury hotel suites, as well as 10 co-op residences. Amenities include a fitness center, business center, and a salon and spa by Frédéric Fekkai. Also included: personal shopping and delivery service, housekeeping and turndown service for bed linens, a dog-walking service, a fleet of custom bicycles, a Bergdorf Goodman store, Jean Georges restaurant and in-room dining, and a lot more.

I elaborated on these two buildings to give you a little idea of what living in a Manhattan luxury co-op can be like. Co-ops entail special privileges.

And yet, as I mentioned, co-ops are on the way to become a thing of the past, and those special privileges now appear more commonly in modern condos.

Conversions from rentals to co-ops nowadays can be counted in the single digits.

In fact, it's common to see buildings being converted not *from* rentals but *into* rentals! Having tenants rather than buyers is still more appealing to many property developers and owners, and Manhattan rental buildings today command the highest monthly rates ever. A great number of buildings, that in the 1970s and 1980s would have been rent-stabilized or rent-controlled, can today demand "fair market" rent.

Here's an interesting example. For many years I've enjoyed a mutually lucrative professional relationship with a company called Metroloft Management, owned by Nathan and Jack Berman. They are the largest developer and owner of rental buildings in Manhattan and they set the modern standard of quality for downtown rental buildings.

Starting with 17 John Street, they gradually assembled an impressive portfolio of former office buildings in the Financial District that today includes 130 William Street, 63 and 67 Wall Street, as well as 20 Exchange Pace and the Stock Market Building located at 20 Broad Street. They converted all these buildings not into co-ops or condos, but into high-end rentals because they're great believers in passive income and regular monthly cash flow.

Metroloft Management is another company that is also respected for providing the highest-quality amenities in their buildings, and for great customer service. They cater to young professionals and offer special incentives to renters, such as one or even two months of free rent to new tenants.

These buildings have many interesting architectural details and unique features. For example, 20 Exchange Place was at one time the highest Art Deco office skyscraper in downtown Manhattan.

I'd like you to be inspired by Metroloft's success and actively seek opportunities to invest in rental properties so you can begin receiving steady passive income and prosper.

Now to get back to the co-op vs condo dichotomy...

When you invest in a co-op, you receive a certain number of stock certificates (shares) of the corporation that owns the building and a lease agreement to one of the units, very similar to the one you get as an apartment renter. The corporation that owns the building becomes your landlord, and the extent of your rights as a tenant is determined largely by the size of your share.

Having invested in a condo, you receive a deed - a document that grants you the ownership of the interior of the unit you've purchased, as well as the interest in the common parts of the building, such as the lobby, elevators, recreation room, and so on.

One thing I can say for co-ops is that they tend to be somewhat less pricey than condominiums. For example, in 2018, the average price of a square foot of co-op space in Manhattan was $1,319, whereas an average square foot in a condo unit went for $1,989.

There are several reasons for this noticeable price difference. One of them is that co-op buildings tend to be older and lack the kind of off-the-charts contemporary niceties available in newer condos. Another is that some of the best new condos today come with decently long tax abatements. This is a great perk for buyers because it allows them to sell these new properties at higher prices. But probably the most important factor that drives down the co-op price per-square-foot is the notorious board approval process, which we'll get to in a New York minute.

Aside from the actual price, whether you own shares of the co-op or a real property unit in a condominium building, you have to consider monthly costs, not including what you pay back to a bank every month.

In a co-op, what you pay every month is known as a "mainte-nance fee." That fee is comprised of two parts: your share of the cost of operating the building and your share of the building's property taxes. You should expect these costs to increase year after year.

That's not all. Whenever your building requires repairs or additional funds for cash reserve, it may require you to pay a certain percentage of total cost, commensurate with your number of shares. That amount can range from a few thousand to tens of thousands of dollars, although you should be able to spread your payment over a period of time ranging from half a year to a year and a half. This is known as a capital assessment.

Monthly payments in a condominium are known as "common charges", and all other things being equal, they tend to be noticeably lower than maintenance fees in a co-op, especially in larger buildings. However, common charges do not include real estate taxes. This is a very important fact to consider when you compare the monthly costs of several possible future homes you're considering. With real estate taxes included, your total yearly spending in a co-op and a condo may, in fact, be comparable.

Unless you're in possession of an extraordinary amount of cash, you are probably going to rely on the "down-payment plus loan" model. That model is applicable to many co-ops and practically all condos, but the rules of the game are somewhat different.

A typical co-op will expect a down-payment of at least 25% to 30%, and in certain cases as much as 50%! And then there are a few co-ops in New York City that will not approve buyers who have to ask a bank for any amount of money.

Another thing you should be aware of when dealing with co-ops is a so-called "liquid assets requirement": the expectation that after you provide the down-payment, you have a certain amount of money left in your bank account. On average, the expectation is that you have at least two years' worth of bank payments and maintenance fees at your disposal. At the higher end, with some of the co-ops you may find out that after making the down-payment you're required, to have the 100% of the cost of the apartment that you've just secured left in your bank account. Or sometimes as much as 300%! Basically, if you want a foot in the door of a very high-end Manhattan co-op, being well-off might just not cut it. You'd better be rich.

It's somewhat easier with condos, where you won't be required to expose the most minute details of your financial situation, or to have ridiculously high equity from the get-go. If a bank approves you for a mortgage with a 20% down-payment, typically that's good enough for becoming a qualified condo buyer.

A co-op is governed by a <u>co-op board</u>, and a condo by a <u>board of directors</u>. Generally speaking, both kinds of boards are elected by all the members, and are responsible for every decision pertaining to managing the day-to-day operations of their properties. The difference is one of clout. The co-op board reigns supreme, wielding almost totalitarian power over the corporation-owned property, and even the shareholders. For example, a co-op board has the right to force a pesky member with a propensity for frequent noisy all-night parties out of the co-op by voting that person to sell their shares back to the corporation.

A board of directors in the condominium has a lot less power, precisely because the board doesn't represent the corporation that owns the property—in this case the resident is the owner of real property, and with that status comes more legal power.

Today, as I'm writing this, I'm checking the newest monthly market report on my second computer screen. The average price of a Manhattan condominium stands at about $3.3 million, whereas the average price of a co-op is $1.4 million. One would assume that all other things being equal, co-ops should outsell the condos by at least 100 percent, but that's not the case. Out of 884 residential units sold in Manhattan this month, 425 are condos and 459 are coops.

Sales of cooperatives priced above $5 million declined by 20% in 2016 and continue to fall. For super-luxury co-ops priced at $20 million and up, sales declined by 25% in the same year. I think the main reason for such a drastic decline in co-op sales is the fact that a condo has an overwhelmingly higher probability of being in a newer building than a co-op. Newer buildings mean newer amenities, and as we know the latest amenities are all the rage nowadays.

Another purely economic reason for the co-op sales decline is that today banks encourage condo purchases and finance 80% of the purchase at a low interest rate. We've seen a 2.5% interest rate on a five-year interest-only mortgage. (**Note:** this percentage is only valid if you buy the home you're going to live in, also referred to as "prime residence"; if you already own a home and are buying a secondary property as an investor, you'll be expected to provide at least a 50% deposit).

Buying a co-op, even for a prime residence, you may be required to provide no less than a 25% to 30% down-payment - but every co-op is different and you should check its minimum down payment requirements. Bank loans for co-ops come with higher interest rates than those for condos.

Finally, a third and most fundamental reason why co-op sales are on the decline is that buying a co-op in Manhattan is a pain in the neck (and that's being polite about it!).

To secure a purchase of shares in a co-op, an investor must meet a strict set of criteria, the most important being their financial situation. The co-op board will definitely demand to see your tax returns. If you'd rather not share your tax return documents with a bunch of complete strangers, then co-op living is not for you, plain and simple.

Within ten days of accepted offer (not made), a co-op buyer must submit an application to the co-op's board of directors, supplemented by a great number of obligatory documents.

Preparing those documents takes a lot longer than 10 days—it could take weeks. You'll have to collect financial reports, reference letters, a letter of commitment from the bank, and so on. It's also recommended that the co-op investors submit a one-page cover letter, using it to present themselves as (to quote one of my Manhattan colleagues) "quiet, boring, and rich." Co-ops are an upper class phenomenon, and the true upper class prefer to keep a low profile and act low-key—so you should tone down anything that you think makes you unique and interesting and pretty much give yourself the blandness and nutritional value of watery British porridge.

Furthermore, when you buy a co-op, you must be interviewed by a co-op board. They'll tell you anything you want to know about the co-op, and in return will ask you a lot of probing questions. If some of the directors don't like what they've learned about you and vote "no", you won't be accepted as a member, even if you may have felt that everybody on the board loved you. In my real estate practice I've seen too many examples of how fickle co-op boards can be.

I remember a situation when the rules of a certain cooperative allowed parents to buy apartments in that building for their children. My client, a high net worth individual, was buying a place for his adult daughter, an NYU student. We asked the seller if there would be a problem with that setup, and received their assurance that we wouldn't experience any. We applied, the co-op shook my client's hand and told him "welcome to our building." The next day he received a rejection letter with no explanation. Co-ops don't have to explain their decisions. They just have the right to say no.

When dealing with a co-op, any small error of judgement can undermine your chances of success.

Another client of mine had their heart set on buying a co-op within Museum Mile in a luxury building with only two apartments per floor. My client loved the place, and she thought she could make it even lovelier if she replaced the old wallpaper in the shared corridor. She wanted to be courteous and ask her future neighbor if this would be acceptable. So, my client just knocked on her door, and even I, with my swift reflexes fine-tuned by decades of real estate broker experience, still didn't react fast enough to stop her!

I should probably mention that this was in a "white-glove" building with an elevator attendant and a doorman who calls the residents to advise them they have visitors before allowing anyone up. (I can almost hear you groaning right now in anticipation of something highly unpleasant.) The door opened and we saw a charming old lady who smiled and told us how happy she'd be to have such a great new neighbor. I was relieved and hoped for the best, but during the interview with co-op board my client was reminded of that event, and the members asked what possessed her to knock at the "forbidden door". She was rejected.

I'm happy to say that within the next two months I helped that client to buy an even nicer apartment—a condo. The experience with the "charming old lady" and the co-op board had freed my client from her romantic notions about owning a co-op in Manhattan.

You can also expect to find some peculiarities in co-op rules.

Yet another client of mine was interested in a co-op in a very small, cozy building in SoHo with only five apartments on five floors. Every resident of the building met my client for the interview and he discovered that once a week, every week he'd be responsible for removing all the garbage from the entire building. Considering that the price for that co-op was $2.8 million, my client decided that as tempting as the prospect of personally handling half a ton of weekly garbage might be, he'd have to respectfully decline the opportunity to join that co-op.

Suppose that you are not concerned with the day-to-day rules of the building because you're not planning to live in it at all: you're an investor looking for a place to lease to a tenant, for passive income. Unfortunately, co-ops rank rather low as investment opportunities of that kind, due to the fact that they are notoriously difficulty about letting owners sublet. You may be allowed to sublet your condo for no longer than one year out of every five. You also need to consider the possibility that the ever-present co-op board may not approve of the person who wishes to lease your apartment from you.

Selling a co-op isn't easy, either. Imagine a situation where you absolutely must sell your apartment, and you find a buyer who's ready to pay the asking price in cash. Awesome! - However, the board rejects the buyer and never explains to you why - but hey, you're more than welcome to bring in the next candidate, who might be equally likely to be rejected! The only thing I can tell you on that subject is that you'd probably be well-advised to not try selling your co-op to a lawyer; many of the co-op boards would never approve a lawyer because lawyers know how to sue and who would want *that*?

Even in order to sublet your co-op, you have to obtain approval from the board - which you may not get. As a rule, courts do not intervene in co-op boards' decisions, even if these decisions are unpopular. As a broker, I wouldn't go so far as to say that I'm adamantly against co-ops. If you come to me as a client and demand, "co-op or bust!" - I'll help you. And of course, if you have the good fortune of owning a co-op and want to get rid of it, I'll also see what I can do for you.

But to me co-ops are not worth the trouble. Setting up a co-op deal may take three months or more of intense labor only for the client to get rejected. All that hard work is wasted, my well-earned pay goes to waste, and my client and I have to start from scratch again. Don't get me wrong: I'm prepared to put in as much effort as necessary to fulfill my clients' wishes, and I enjoy every aspect of my profession, but there comes a point where hard work ends and inefficiency begins.

That's why I think it's more reasonable today to invest in condos than in co-ops. All other things being equal as a condo owner, you'll enjoy lower interest rates on your mortgage and lower monthly maintenance fees—and as I mentioned, you'll find it a lot easier to buy, sell, or rent your property.

There are, however, a few reasons to choose a co-op over a condo!

As we discussed, co-ops tend to be a lot cheaper than condos, and for that reason they often don't require much of a mortgage. Incorporation comes with tax incentives, and owning a share in a co-op is no exception: Federal and State laws provide considerable tax deductions for real estate and loan interest to co-op owners, but that doesn't apply to all situations: some co-ops do not meet the criteria that allow such deductions, so I advise you to be *extremely* attentive as you carry out your due diligence. As I've already mentioned, the number of co-ops in Manhattan significantly exceeds the number of condos, so with co-ops you have a wider choice.

And finally, one thing to be said for co-ops is that their disadvantages are an extension of their advantages, so seeing that in a positive light, if you do get accepted by the board members, it's as if you're offered a membership in a highly exclusive private club. Your co-op will not accept "just anybody from the street" as your neighbor, and it will guarantee a certain extra level of privacy, security, and comfort. Some co-ops are so exclusive that it's practically impossible to get into them, unless you're a member of high society or belong to a certain category of people.

If you've just concluded that you have to be rich and famous to get approved by a co-op board, you're wrong. A person can be a rock star, a movie star, or a billionaire, and still get rejected from a co-op! You can be even a real-estate mogul personally and a co-op may still decide you're not good enough. Don't believe me? In 2009, a certain gentleman named Jeff T. Blau was brutally rejected by the co-op board of 820 5th Avenue in 2009. He offered $31 million for an apartment. The co-op refused the cash. Blau happens to be the Chief Executive Officer of The Related Companies, the team responsible for developing the Time Warner Center and Hudson Yards, among many other major urban transformation projects! He also oversees a portfolio of subsidiaries that include such fitness brands as Equinox, Blink, and Soul Cycle. Jeff T. Blau didn't just fail the interview with the board of directors - he was *denied* the interview.

Only in New York.

If you've ever been rejected by a co-op board, allow me to make you feel better about it. You're in good company! Here's a partial list of well-known individuals who didn't make it either:

Madonna, the "Queen of Pop"; Ronald Perlman, owner of McAndrews & Forbes and, at $12 billion, the 26th richest person in America; Calvin Klein, the famous fashion designer; His Highness Sheik Hamad bin Jassim bin Jaber Al-Thani, the ex-prime minister of Qatar, who is also the owner of Harrods - and a few other famous names, such as Cameron Diaz, Mariah Carey, Diane Keaton, Gloria Vanderbilt, Melanie Griffith, Antonio Banderas and Cher; the list goes on.

All or almost all of these "beautiful people" were rejected by the boards of just a handful of buildings. The "usual suspects" are: The Majestic, The Dakota, The Langham, The San Remo, 740 Park Avenue, and 820 5th Avenue.

Co-op boards are allowed to reject a prospective buyer for any legal reason. Since they are also not legally obligated to disclose the actual reason for their rejection, some co-op boards may clandestinely reject a person for any reason at all.

Other possible reasons that may lead to one being rejected by a co-op board: pets (even if the place claims that pets are welcome, *your* pet may not be); you're a professional musician or a music teacher - or simply somebody who plays the piano, heavy metal guitar, or drums for your own enjoinment (as well as that of the neighbors); you look too athletic...like someone who may be lifting (and dropping) weights at home; you're interested in a secondary residence (a pied-à-terre); you have a home-based business; you're a recognizable celebrity with massive following (including the ever-present paparazzi, who may disturb other people in the building)—you get the picture.

The notorious exclusiveness of the super-co-ops I've listed a few paragraphs above actually hurts their sales. The Dakota, designed by architect Henry Janeway Hardenbergh (also famous for The Plaza Hotel), and developed by the revolutionary real estate mogul Edward Cabot Clark, was marketed as New York's first-ever rental apartment building for the rich back in 1884, a time when only the poor lived in apartments and the rich lived in mansions. Eventually, it was converted into a co-op in 1961 and became the home for such cultural icons as Lauren Bacall, Boris Karloff, Jose Ferrer and Rosemary Clooney, Ruth Ford, Roberta Flack, Leonard Bernstein, Rudolf Nureyev, Jack Palance, William Inge, Judy Garland, John Lennon and Yoko Ono, and so on—a very long list of famous people lucky enough to have been accepted by the co-op board, but not nearly as long as the list of equally famous but *unlucky* people *rejected* by it.

Notwithstanding the building's aura of glory and exclusivity, it's not doing too well from the sales standpoint. There are currently six luxury co-op dwellings on the market in The Dakota. All but one have been on the market for a few years now, and they keep dropping their prices a few million dollars at a time. The Dakota is currently a place to get some terrific real estate deals...that is, if you get approved by the co-op board.

Now that you've got the lay of the land, I'd like to provide a little clarification about two kinds of property ownership where separating lines between condo and co-op are blurred.

"Condop" (sometimes also spelled as condo-op) is a contraction of "condo" and "co-op", and it describes a scenario in which a corporation owns several residential units in a condominium, and sells its shares to multiple people who, as shareholders of the corporation, receive the right to use individual units.

Condops are rare. You can be a real estate investor in Manhattan all your life and not once see a condop. In practically all situations, the co-op owns an entire <u>residential</u> part of the building, while the remaining "condo" part represents retail or office space. The entire "condop" approach was nothing but a clever workaround against a pesky provision in one of the sections of old tax law that penalized the co-ops if more than 20% of its building was used for non-residential purposes. The law has since been amended, so there's no need for new condops today.

The **"sponsored apartment"** is a relic of the 1980s. During the boom of rental-to-co-op conversions, renters were offered the choice of either becoming new co-op members or remaining renters. When people preferred to rent, their apartments were not included in the co-op and remained under the ownership of the development company that converted the building. When renters of such apartments move out, the apartment might become available for sale by the sponsor—that is to say by the original development company. Sponsored apartments usually represent a good opportunity to a buyer, because that's how you can buy a "condo in the middle of a co-op" and enjoy all the best things the building has to offer without having to pass the board interview! (You may also appreciate the additional advantage of a lower down-payment.)

Getting back to the "garden variety" co-ops and condos, there are a lot of similarities between the two types of property co-ownership. In co-ops and condominiums alike, there's a property manager who is hired by the board. A board of directors, whether in co-op or condominium, can consist of up to five people, including a president, a secretary, and a treasurer. But often the responsibilities are merged and one person can fulfill the functions of president and secretary - and sometimes there's just one, often tyrannical, person who sits on the board of directors of a co-op or a condo.

If you want to buy additional square footage, or for example build a roof over the outdoor terrace - in a condominium you'd need to buy the "Common Area License." This is done through negotiating with the board of directors. In a similar situation as a member of a co-op, you would need to buy additional shares of the corporation.

Whether it's a co-op or a condo, the building must have an alteration agreement, as well as by-laws that define the building rules. These rules must be enacted and enforced - and to be changed, all members of the co-op or condo board of directors must vote. As a member of the board of directors in my building over the last decade, I must tell you that such voting can turn downright Shakespearean if the discussion turns to such controversial subjects as what flowers to use for lobby decoration.

Selling, buying, and leasing residential units in condominium buildings are subject to approval from a board of directors, exactly like in co-ops. But that's exactly where crucial differences between condos and co-ops become obvious. When it comes to this type of decision, the voting in condominiums is usually fast, smooth, and unanimous, and the deal gets approved.

Why? Well, theoretically, in the course of 30 days when the buyer and seller present the documents to the board, condominiums, just like co-ops, can exercise the so-called right of first refusal. The board of directors can say no to a buyer, seller, or a prospective renter. But they rarely do so. That's because if you're selling your condo, and your board of directors doesn't approve the buyer, or finds the price too low, they're legally obligated to buy your condo from you! Usually they don't have the funds for such purchase, so the buyer just gets approved.

If you want to sublet your apartment, you must have that decision documented by a sublease agreement. As a rule, both condominium and co-op boards of directors hold the right to allow the sublease to take place or not. However, should a condo board decide for whatever reason to not let you sublease your property, they would be legally bound to rent it from you.

Co-ops, on the other hand, are not obligated to buy anything or rent anything from anyone, so they can pretty much say no to whomever whenever they damn well please.

I say, let 'em enjoy it while it lasts because co-ops are a dying breed, the vestige of the Gilded Age. The "Millennials" and "Generation Z" just won't put up with that kind of elitism.

And Manhattan is not likely to see another co-op creation boom similar to the one that happened at the end of 1980.

CHAPTER IV: TOWNHOUSES AND BROWNSTONES

How many total buildings are in Manhattan? The short (but correct) answer: nobody knows.

What? In our age of GPS and proliferation of data we can't count a number of buildings on a small island? It turns out we can't because buildings are so ephemeral! It's as if they're made of dreams, not brick, wood, steel, and concrete. Dozens of buildings are demolished in Manhattan every year, soon forgotten, gone without a trace. They don't even have to be old to be demolished.

For example, 101 Murray Street, designed by Haines Lundberg Waehler, existed only between 1983 and 2006. It was an interesting-looking 10-story building, but it was ruthlessly demolished to give place to the much more impressive 111 Murray Street. Real estate is unsentimental.

The longer answer can be based on the Fiscal Year 2018 Final Assessment Roll, compiled by the city. According to that document, in 2017 there were 147,754 parcels of developable land in Manhattan, to the full market value of $ 450,675,117,779, of which 4,577 were vacant lots.

Each condominium unit counts as a separate lot. There were 94,570 condominiums in Manhattan in 2017. If we take 60 condominiums per building as an approximate average, you get about 1,576 total condo buildings in Manhattan. This leaves us with 53,184 non-condominium buildings. If we add together this number and the number of condominium buildings and deduct the number of vacant lots (53,184 + 1,576) - 4577 you get 50,183 total buildings in Manhattan.

And that's as close to the precise number as we can get. But how many of these are brownstones? And what about townhouses?

It's easier with townhouses. There are 2,084 single-family houses, 1,823 two-family houses, and 1,471 three-family houses, and that will give us the incomplete total of 5,378. My guess would be that at least 2/3 of them are brownstones but what exactly *are* brownstones? And, come to think of it, what are townhouses?

Historically, a townhouse is an urban dwelling for a noble family that usually lives in one or more mansions in the country and comes to stay in their comparatively modest but still luxurious dwelling in the city for a brief period of time, or for an opera season. Such houses would require several floors, with one or more floors allocated for servant quarters.

For our purposes, today's **townhouse** can be defined simply as a multistory urban house.

A townhouse in New York typically occupies a fairly small parcel of land. They are usually 3-6 stories high with no elevator, built from brick, and with stone-clad facade.

Across the entire United States, the stones used to decorate townhouses is often a light-gray color. The highest quality gray stone, known under names of Bedford Limestone, Indiana Limestone, or Salem Limestone, had been quarried in south-central Indiana, between the towns of Bloomington and Bedford.

In New York City though, more often than everywhere else in the country, rather than using limestone, the architects and builders historically preferred to use sandstone to decorate townhouses. That type of sandstone can be recognized by its beautiful reddish-brown hue, and most of it had been ferried to New York from the quarries near New Brunswick and Passaic, New Jersey.

So, a **brownstone** is simply a townhouse decorated with that type of sandstone. What makes things more fun is that townhouses in Manhattan are often painted, and the number of colors defies imagination. I've seen a bubble-gum pink townhouse with my own eyes. Some townhouses are so drastically painted one could swear they'd glow in the dark. (What's violet and green and red all over? A townhouse in Manhattan!) Okay, I'm exaggerating, but only slightly.

In reality, color patterns for townhouses are chosen by individual owners, and the colors tend to be uniformly applied to the entire building. But sometimes you can come across some intriguing color choices.

As we know, Manhattan is chock-full of historic neighborhoods, and townhouses and brownstones are often predominate in such neighborhoods, which sort of makes sense when you stop to think about it because townhouses and brownstones in this classic Manhattan style are no longer being built. A landmark neighborhood is easily recognizable by its street signs; they're not green, but reddish-brown. Many townhouses feature bay windows - rounded windows protruding from the building built in such a way that looking through that window you can view the street from many angles. Imagine having such a window in your townhouse, overlooking Central Park or Riverside Park!

There are many townhouses on the Upper West Side, the Upper East Side and Greenwich Village - neighborhoods and streets with long, interesting histories. Some are 70 to 100 years old or older. Every now and then you can even come across a renovated 200-plus-year-old townhouse for sale in Manhattan, if you're fortunate.

Townhouses are usually anywhere between 15 and 30 feet in width, with the average width around 20 feet. Some of the original townhouses are used as mini-apartment buildings and may include anywhere from 4 to 20 apartments.

Probably the most remarkable townhouse investment over the last few years was the 2018 purchase of the late banker and philanthropist David Rockefeller's 40-feet wide, 40-storied Upper East Side mansion at 146 East 65th Street for $20 million,

$12.5 cheaper than the original asking price. The buyer, incorporated as 146 East 65 LLC, provided a 50% down-payment and obtained the mortgage from Wells Fargo for the remaining half. The 9,777-square-feet city mansion includes eight bedrooms, eight fireplaces, a temperature-controlled wine vault, a 3,000-square-foot landscaped garden, and a skylight on the top floor. A beautiful place.

Styles of Townhouses

Most Manhattan townhouses fall within one of several distinct architectural styles:

The Federal Style, popular in the early 19th century, is characterized by small-scale and modest ornamentation. Such townhouses are smaller, only 2 or 3 stories on a tiny parcel of land, and you can easily recognize them by attic windows cut through the slanted roof.

Later, around 1830 to 1850, the **Greek Revival** style became more popular. Look for townhouses with Doric or Corinthian columns next to their entrances.

From the 1840s through 1860s, the **Gothic Revival** style came into prominence, featuring pointed arches, stone and cast-iron ornamentations, and an air of medievalism.

The **Italianate** style (1840s to 1870s and even newer), recognizable by the combination of horizontal stone "bands" decorating the façade, as well as ornamental cornices over the windows and around the roof. Another interesting style also popular around that time is known as **Anglo-Italianate**, which featured one or two floors decorated with brownstones. They look almost exactly like Italianate buildings, but the remaining floors are not decorated at all. All the way up to the roof they're just bare bricks or small stones that look like bricks.

The **Second Empire** style, popular in 1860-1875, combines stone bands and elaborate cornices of Italianate style with slanted roofs and dormer windows of the Federal style. The **Neo Greek** style, which coincided timewise, is just like the Second Empire with added Doric or Corinthian columns from Greek Revival, *sans* the slanted roof and dormer windows. (The combinations are getting somewhat complicated, as you can see.)

The **Queen Anne** style, from around 1870s till 1890s, is like a sudden burst of jazz after the classical music of the previous styles. Highly eclectic, it combines every feature of every style, with rough and smooth stones used for decoration, stoops bent at 90-degree angles, basement windows, bay windows and architraves, friezes, and gables with rounded elements in the plane, rectangular cross-sections and sometimes even triangular windows. These townhouses somehow manage to represent a stylistically unified whole, and are highly valued.

Between 1870 and the 1890s, as a push back against this wildness, townhouse architects worked in the **Romanesque Revival** style characterized by rounded arches and stern simplicity, slightly offset by asymmetrical structure of the façade.

The 1890s through 1930s were marked by the boom of townhouse construction and its gradual decline, with four styles coinciding: **Renaissance Revival** (taller buildings with balustrades, arches and balconies); **Colonial Revival** (very much like Federal, but even smaller and more minimalist, very symmetrical); **Beaux-Art** (highly elaborate, ornamented neoclassicism; a townhouse in that style looks more like a town*palace*, and will cost you accordingly); and **English Neoclassical** (think "ancient Roman villa in the middle of New York, except with a colder, rational Nordic demeanor in the place of Italian exuberance").

Most of the townhouses I've worked on were built around the time of the first phases of New York City subway construction. The entire island of Manhattan lies atop huge slabs of granite bedrock. When the first subway tunnels were excavated, large pieces and blocks of granite were given to house builders practically free—a much more efficient way to get rid of that granite than transporting it off the island. Builders used these chunks of super-hard rock for the foundations of the brownstones.

Whenever I see such granite foundations, I recognize a sturdy and most valuable townhouse, and I know that I will sell it. A townhouse is priced even higher if it has unusually fine architectural or interior details, a great view of a park or a river, or a particularly imposing stoop. And, as always, the closeness to public transportation contributes to the price.

Some Manhattan townhouses offer something truly special. Older townhouses often had adjacent stables for horses and carriage houses built on the ground floor. Very few of these houses still exist, and like all rarities they're highly coveted by buyers. Owners often convert such adjacent structures into grand "ballroom-style" garden lobbies - or into garages. Some of these buyers, not surprisingly, own a collection of luxury or sports cars.

The stand-up comedian Jerry Seinfeld, for example, is an avid automobile enthusiast and collector. In 2002 he purchased a townhouse on the Upper West Side with a carriage house and converted it into a two-story super-garage with 4 separate car rooms, an elevator, a club room with a pool table, a kitchenette and bathroom, and a large office. The place hosts the rotating roster of Jerry's collection of 46 Porsche automobiles. A high-tech HVAC unit on the roof maintains the ideal garage temperature, and whenever Seinfeld finds himself away from home and feels particularly nostalgic, he can open a special app on his mobile phone and view the real-time video feed of the entire interior of his garage and the street outside.

There are approximately 300 townhouses with garages in Manhattan today. The city has changed its laws, and today you can't add a curb cut anymore, so adding a garage to a townhouse is no longer an option. Therefore, those townhouses that do include garages are highly sought-after, and cost considerably more.

An interesting special type of property that I believe every investor must be educated about is a mixed-use townhouse. We speak about mixed use when a townhouse includes an office or a retail component. In some cases, zoning allows - or even demands - the mixed use.

Sometimes zoning also allows special signage. Walking down a beautiful Upper East Side street, you may notice that in one block filled entirely with townhouses there's not a single business sign - and then in the very next block every other house has a sign for a lawyer or an accountant or a doctor, or a music school. That's the effect of zoning: in the block where you see these signs, zoning allows mixed use for townhouses, and any professional can place their silver, gold, or copper identity plaque on the side of the house or even in the adjacent mini-garden.

If you're a New Yorker, when I ask you to visualize a townhouse, you're most likely to imagine one located on a street. But there are townhouses on avenues, too. In almost all such townhouses there are stores in the ground floors, or sometimes even in the couple of lower floors, or in the basement. Avenue townhouses containing stores on three levels are not unknown, either. This can only be done when zoning allows such use. The reason property owners can decide to take that approach is known as **"highest and best use"** - an important term in real estate which means, basically, "whatever can bring you and others the highest value".

As an aside, so-called vertical shopping (stores on many floors of the same building,) has not been very wide-spread in Manhattan. We know several vertical stores that existed for decades - Macy's, Sachs 5th Avenue, Bergdorf Goodman - but these used to be rare exceptions from the predominance of street-level retail. Today we're beginning to see more vertical shopping: Time Warner Center, Lord and Taylor, Barneys - as well as Nordstrom, which will soon open at Central Park Tower.

There are townhouses in Manhattan currently allocated for completely nonresidential use. The best and most notable example is the Henry Clay Frick House. On his deathbed, the owner bequeathed that house to the public as a museum. Today it's known as the Frick Collection and the Frick Art Reference Library.

The Cartier Building

Probably the most famous Manhattan townhouse-related legend is the story of the Cartier Building on the corner of 52nd Street and 5th Avenue. During the last quarter of 19th century, the area was filled with mansions owned mostly by the Vanderbilt family.

The Vanderbilts also owned most of the land in the area, and were very careful whom they sold it to. It was their greatest concern to not let any merchants into the neighborhood so it remained quiet, dignified, and upscale. In 1905, they sold the lot of land on the southeast corner of 52nd Street and 5th Avenue to railroad investor and shipping magnate Morton Freeman Plant, who immediately proceeded to build a posh limestone townhouse there, designed in Neo-Renaissance style by architect Richard W. Gibson. The townhouse was surrounded by an intricate iron fence with a deep areaway between the house and the street, to further protect Morton Plant's privacy.

In 1911, the city made life harder for mansion owners, ordering them to eliminate fences, gardens, stoops, porte-cocheres, and protruding ornamentation - anything encroaching on the areas given to public sidewalks. Morton Plant had to get rid of his iron fence and areaway, and now any passerby could spy on the magnate through his living room window. But Plant firmly planted himself in his fortress, and stubbornly refused to sell it to anyone. The magnate loved his townhouse.

Despite the Vanderbilts' efforts, trade gradually invaded the neighborhood, starting with the French jewelry house Cartier, which in 1907 built the very first business building in the area, at

712 5th Avenue near 56th Street. Morton Plant's young wife Mae frequented their store and fell in love with Cartier's most valuable creation, a two-strand pearl necklace. She loved the necklace almost as much as her husband loved his townhouse. She visited the store just to admire the glorious necklace like a work of art in a gallery. The price of the necklace seemed impossible, even to the wife of a railroad magnate: $1 million.

In 1917, Louis and Pierre Cartier offered Morton Plant a deal: the pearl necklace in exchange for his townhouse. That was a tough choice, but to Morton Plant's honor, his love for his wife prevailed. He said yes and moved to a new, even more luxurious townhouse on East 86th street, designed by Guy Lowell.

That's how Cartier became the owner of this famous building and Mae Plant got her necklace.

Was it a fair deal? Let's find out! The average yearly inflation throughout the century had been 3.07%. This means that in 1917 $1 million equals $21,252,068.97 today. A four-story Neo-Renaissance townhouse in Manhattan on 5th avenue and 52nd street, for a little over $21 million? Morton Plant made a bad bargain! But of course, you can't quantify love.

My clients often ask me which is a smarter investment: a condo or a townhouse. Let me give you a little background information so that together we can arrive at the best answer.

Quarterly real estate taxes paid in NY are an important issue relevant to qualifying property as a high-quality investment. New York City's Department of Finance makes a tax assessment of every property by January 5th of each year, and has four tax classes for real estate.

The Four Tax Classes

Class 1 includes most residential properties of up to three units. This means that one-family, two-family and three-family townhouses, as well as most condominiums fall within this class.

Class 2 includes all other property that is primarily residential. 4-family townhouses, condominiums that have more than three stories, and *all co-operatives* fall within this tax class.

Classes 3 and 4 include "property with utility company-owned equipment" and "all commercial or industrial property that is not in the other three tax classes", respectively.

The yearly tax assessment sets the amount of taxes to be paid for Class 1 property at 8%. By comparison, properties that belong to Classes 2 through 4 are tax-assessed at 45% percent! So, a Class 1 property that has the assessed cost of $1 million would have a tax assessment of $80,000, whereas similar-priced Class 2 property would be tax-assessed at $450,000.

Don't get spooked before I explain. This tax assessment doesn't mean that every year you have to pay 8% or 45% of the cost of your property in taxes. It's just the overall percentage of your property that is taxable. The taxes are actually additionally calculated based on that. What Class 1 property owners paid in 2017 was 19.991% tax on the 8% of property, whereas Class 2 property owners paid 12.892% tax on the value of 45% of their property. Your accountant would probably better explain to you the details of how *this* was calculated.

How does the Department of Finance make these yearly estimations? There are three parameters.

1. Sales comparison: The Department of Finance analyzes sales of similar recently sold properties to assess the correct price of the given property.
2. Cost: The Department of Finance compares the combined value of the land on which the property is located with how much it would cost to build that property on that lot today.
3. Income capitalization: the Department of Finance estimates what income could be earned through the highest and best use of this property.

A small exception to these rules is the estimation of value of cooperatives and condominiums. State law requires that the Department of Finance estimate the value of co-ops and condominiums as if they were rental buildings. Therefore, their value is assessed based on the probable monthly rent of these properties, even though they're actually not for rent. The advantage of this law is that even if you sold or bought a condo or a co-op at a much higher price, the tax on this property won't skyrocket because rent value grows slower than sales prices.

Otherwise, at some tipping point the rent would become so unrealistically high that no one would rent the property.

Additionally, there are limits imposed by State Law that regulate the change in assessment of property value the Department of Finance is allowed to make on the yearly basis. For Class 1 properties, the change in assessment cannot exceed 6% per year or 20% in five years. For Class 2 properties, if there are fewer than 11 units, such change cannot exceed 8% per year or 30% in five years. The rules for properties of 11 units or more are slightly more complicated and involve "phasing-in" over 5 years of any change in assessed value. (Class 3 has no limits on how the value change can be calculated, and Class 4 must also be "phased-in" over 5 years...as complicated as this may seem).

Based on the above from a tax perspective, assuming exactly the same price of a hypothetical property, a townhouse or condominium represent better investments than a co-op because even though your co-op is assessed as a rental, a whopping 45% of its estimated value is taxable. Also from the same point of view, a condominium is a better investment than a townhouse because the taxable 8% of the townhouse value is based on its sales price, whereas for a condo it's estimated based on the rent, which can be considerably lower.

Something else that comes into play are tax abatements. As a rule, there are no tax abatements on historic townhouses because in an overwhelming majority of cases tax abatements are applied to new developments. You can get a condo with a tax abatement if it has been developed within the last couple of decades.

The cost of keeping a townhouse may seem prohibitive to many, and from that point of view a condo is also an easier investment. The average size of a Manhattan townhouse is about 4,500 square feet. With a condo or co-op of the same size, the average cost of maintenance per square foot in Manhattan is $2.5, which will get you $11,250 in common charges per year. As a townhouse owner, your cost of maintaining the entire building would probably be more like $15,000 to $20,000 per year. You'd have to pay for repairs and upkeep of your townhouse - drain the flooded basement, fix the burst pipe, fix the roof, or paint the façade just the right hue of bright orange you imagined in your dreams - even though you can and should write off a certain portion of that cost every year when you fill out your tax documents.

Besides annual real estate taxes that are due quarterly, there are other forces at play that can make a townhouse a more interesting investment for you than a condo. Over the last couple of decades, we've witnessed considerably higher growth in prices of townhouses, even compared to condominiums. The prices of early 19th century townhouses jumped 20% to 30% per year. Anything that's rare is valued, and old-school townhouses, obviously, are not being built today. But they are being renovated, just as I described in the previous paragraph - which, combined with their relative rarity explains their steady and fast growth in price. You can always find a buyer for a townhouse, because townhouses are beautiful and rare.

It becomes a little more interesting if you've bought a townhouse and conducted a multimillion-dollar renovation, which may have doubled its value. Or suppose you demolished an old townhouse and built a modern building on that land. The new property may have five times the value of the old one, and as a full property owner you can do all kinds of interesting things with it, such as converting it into a condo and selling some of the units or renting them out. In this case, you stayed within Class 1 so your increase in taxable value still can't go above 6% per year. Of course, you've spent a ton of money and effort on construction work, probably had to obtain the new Certificate of Occupancy, and so on, but if you managed to buy the townhouse at a low price in the first place, you're still going to come out a winner. You probably can't do it on so grand a scale with condos, so from that point of view if you have a sizable enough budget for bold action, a townhouse may be a better investment than a condo, even from the point of view of the annual real estate taxes. And you wouldn't have to ask a board of directors permission to do anything with your property, as long as everything you do is in compliance with the NY building code and work is filed and signed off by the DOB (Department of Buildings).

A townhouse allows you much more privacy. There are no neighbors living in the same building, and you can crank your sound system up to eleven if you'd like. UPS won't leave the package with the doorman because - well, because you don't have a doorman. Unless you'd like to install a computer-assisted "virtual doorman" with special instructions for FedEx and UPS. And that device is costly.

To summarize: townhouse ownership will cost more and be associated with higher responsibilities for you as the investor. However, the much faster growth in prices of townhouses, more freedom of action, and an abundance of prospective buyers can make a townhouse the more appealing and more profitable choice over a condo.

Ultimately advantages and disadvantages can be found in any type of property ownership, and to a large degree it is a question of balancing the pros and cons of each individual opportunity. I'd like to encourage you to do exhaustive due diligence if you're considering an investment in a townhouse - especially if you fell in love with the house and the neighborhood. And you must have the full support from a team of experts. We'll talk about that in the corresponding chapter of this book.

As I wrap up this chapter I'd like to share a small personal anecdote. Back in 1990s, I helped a client sell a great townhouse on Park Avenue and 39th Street for $800,000. That deal had no other broker: I represented both the seller and the buyer. The new owner lived in Westchester and bought the townhouse, planning to move into Manhattan with his family. He was a real estate developer by occupation - and by true calling! - so he conducted a complete "gut renovation" of the townhouse, built two extra floors, and installed the elevator.

Then he talked to his wife about it, and *together* they decided not to move to Manhattan after all. They had a nice place in Westchester, their kids studied in quality schools there, so what was the point of moving to the city? What the hell was he thinking?! He came back to me and asked me to sell the same townhouse for him. That's how, only a year and a half after the first deal, we sold the house for the asking price or $1.9 million (that's 237.5% of the original price in 18 months, folks).

Suddenly the prices for Manhattan townhouses went through the roof (pun intended, my apologies.) Two years later, the new owner of that townhouse came back to me and asked me to sell it for him. He was into tech and kept himself entertained by adding a thermostat here, a set of speakers there, until the old townhouse was transformed into one of the first "smart townhouses" in Manhattan. We sold it for $3.7 million: that's 362.5% of the original price in three and a half years!

Today I estimate that the value of that townhouse as *at least* $9 million. I wouldn't say no to selling that townhouse for the fourth time. Unfortunately for me, the current owner has been holding onto his precious townhouse for over 15 years now.

But if we learned anything from the legendary purchase of the Cartier Building, it's this: any townhouse can be bought when the buyer names the right price.

Jokes aside, we'll discuss the phenomenon of "not-for-sale" real estate, which is actually *quite for sale*, later in this book. It's known as "shadow inventory," and there's plenty of it in Manhattan for a knowledgeable investor.

Chapter V: Commercial Real Estate

When I say "commercial real estate in Manhattan", what's the first thing that comes to mind? If you're local, you're most likely thinking of office space - did I guess correctly? There are, in fact, many additional facets to commercial real estate than there are to residential properties, and each comes with unique challenges and advantages.

Office real estate is just one of these facets - but it's as good as any to start with. No worries, in this chapter we'll cover them all.

Office Space

We live in New York at a time when America is experiencing an economic boom with its tech-based economy, where office workers need fast internet, tech-friendly spaces, conference rooms, and vast open work areas. The age of cubicles and tightly-shut offices is in the past. Today, people enjoy the connectedness of being able to see each other as they work together. This new trend offers interesting challenges, as well as intriguing opportunities for real estate investors. You may find a buyer for a much larger square footage of office space - in that case you'd better have enough capital to invest on a much more massive scale than was typical only a few years ago.

The most interesting concept that truly upturned office real estate in New York (as well as everywhere else, really!) was established by the company called WeWork. I am lucky enough to know Joel Schreiber, the earliest investor and co-owner of WeWork, and also one of the largest real estate investors and landlords in New York. Today, WeWork is valued at $20 billion, and it brought in more than a billion dollars in revenue in the past year.

The intriguing thing about WeWork is that they're equally comfortable with buying and renting large office buildings, and in both cases, they lease it to people operating within the mentality of the "shared economy" - that is, the notion of saving money by sharing resources. Uber, Lyft, Airbnb - all these businesses are based on this underlying philosophy. In fact, WeWork and Airbnb recently teamed up to bring business travelers to WeWork offices.

The stock market is rather in love with WeWork, and on the wave of their IPO, WeWork managed to buy the Lord and Taylor building on 5th Avenue for $850 million (the store remains in the building, but it's now WeWork's commercial tenant). WeWork also bought Meetup for $200 million.

The majority of WeWork clients are freelancers, entrepreneurs or small businesses looking for customizable office space and for the community fostered by the WeWork hub.

WeWork is currently located in 59 cities and has 275 office spaces worldwide. The company also launched a new program, WeLive - community-focused micro-apartments based on the WeWork model. Currently there are only two WeLive locations, and one of them is in Manhattan, at 110 Wall Street.

It's difficult, though by no means impossible, to compete against the likes of WeWork - but I'd like you to find inspiration in their success. Nobody had ever heard of WeWork only a few years ago, and today they are huge and virtually omnipresent. If they could succeed in the field of commercial real estate so fast and on such a massive scale - why couldn't you? At the very least, you can consider them an excellent prospective buyer of office property - if sometime in the future you find yourself having a tasty morsel of office space on your hands.

Retail Spaces

It would be fair to say that traditional brick and mortar retail is in crisis today. In fact, *"Retailpocalypse"* would probably be the right term for the situation - maybe I should trademark the word? The giant meteorite that smashed into the dinosaur world of traditional retail, and is currently driving the species to slow but inevitable extinction, has a name: the internet. Needless to say, this crisis is profoundly affecting retail real estate as well.

In January 2016, Invesco Real Estate paid $112 million for a 4,465-square-foot retail condominium at 139 Spring Street, occupied by Chanel. That's $25,084.99 per square foot.

Just to give you a little perspective what this figure means - the average sales price of retail space in Manhattan in 2016 was approximately $1,167.77, so Invesco paid 21.48 times the average price! This off-market deal probably took some time to arrange, and may have felt like a good idea at the time. SoHo is home to thousands of retail stores, and most of world's top retail brands feel they must have a brick-and-mortar store there. I'm sure the analysts at Invesco did their homework and concluded that Chanel would never want to move out, and even if it did, the place would immediately find a new occupant willing to pay the top dollar in rent. They may have been correct in their calculation, at least in short term, but I still can't help visualizing the sellers of the condo, Spring & Wooster, LLC, laughing and high-fiving each other all the way to the bank. Prices on retail space in Manhattan are dropping like a TV set hurled out of a skyscraper window. Even in the areas of the city where retail was abundant and expensive, the traditional brick-and-mortar retail is going the way of the dodo.

The shocking truth is that today people visit physical stores increasingly less often, instead preferring to do their shopping online.

Let me give you some figures. The percentage of online shoppers in 2017 was estimated at 9.1% vs 90.1% brick-and-mortar purchases. This sounds like a drop in the ocean, but what if I told you it amounts to $453.5 billion in yearly revenue, and that 6,985 brick and mortar stores announced their closure in 2017, which is about 300% compared to 2016? By 2022, at least 17% of all purchases in the United States will be made online, and we may conservatively expect the number of brick-and-mortar retail location closures to count in ten - if not hundreds - of thousands per year. By the way, at least 40% of online purchases today are made using a smartphone, and it's projected to be over 55% by 2022.

If at the turn of the millennium someone told you that a phone would replace a staple of American consumerism such as the suburban shopping mall, wouldn't you have found that patently absurd! A phone going up against a shopping mall? The two things aren't even remotely in the same category! You can buy a phone at a shopping mall! And yet, here we are…

Obviously, Amazon is the big chef in this kitchen, currently making 44% of all E-Commerce sales in the United States, and continually expanding its influence. The escalating shift to online shopping has resulted in a drastic decline of revenue for brick-and-mortar stores; however, their rent continues to increase, which results in more and more stores reaching the tipping point. They either innovate and go full-on E-Commerce, or find a cheaper location and scale down, or - increasingly more likely - simply go out of business. In all three cases, they move out.

That's why today we don't have to walk longer than a couple of blocks down any street in Manhattan before we see a "for rent" sign where a cool retail store existed for many years previously.

Will the brick-and-mortar retail business make a big comeback? It'd be easy to say "no, I don't think so." Actually, something is brewing. Amazon started experimenting by opening brick-and-mortar locations. Apple consistently increases its brick-and-mortar presence, both by adding new stores and expanding existing ones. Samsung opened a flagship location, known as "Samsung 837", in the Meatpacking District at 837 Washington Street, in a six-story building developed and owned by Taconic Investment Partners and Thor Equities. It's not really a retail store: you can't buy any Samsung tech gadgets or home appliances there. Instead, it's an arena for immersive technological experiences that involves virtual reality, music, and oversized screens to build curiosity and loyalty to the Samsung brand. The entire experiential center is a "marketing architectural object".

The now-defunct "Made by Google" pop-up store on the corner of Spring and Mercer proved to be an interesting experiment as well. "Cadillac House" at 330 Hudson Street combines a car showroom with a Cadillac-branded art gallery and restaurant. Just yesterday it was announced that Union Investment Real Estate GmbH, a German investment firm had finally put the deal in place for a long-awaited "Intersect by Lexus" - a three-story "experiential showroom" on 17,000 square feet at 412 West 14th Street, that will include a coffee shop, a restaurant, a gallery, and an event space.

Starbucks recently opened its largest-ever coffee shop in New York's Chelsea, a 20,000 square foot roastery, serving "coffee as theater".

Children's retail is also trying things out. Dylan's Candy Bar and Sugar Factory are among the stores that bring the experience to the center of their retail philosophy. It's worth mentioning that some of the pioneers of experiential retail for children, such as the famous and now-defunct F.A.O. Schwartz and most recently Toys 'R' Us, are among the unfortunate losers.

With some inevitable tweaking, the new model of brick-and-mortar retail will probably be discovered, and if the current incipient trend is to be trusted, it will have something to do with experiencing the brands via each of the five senses - the high-tech version of the model that was probably pioneered, in its own idiosyncratic way, by Abercrombie and Fitch.

But this new concept has not been quite formulated yet. In the meantime, the landlords will have no other choice but to continue dropping prices for retail locations in Manhattan, and we'll probably never see retail business the way it used to be. We're also aren't likely to see a hundred-plus-million-dollar deal on the retail space, like the purchase of the Chanel store, anytime in the foreseeable future.

With retail real estate prices falling and empty storefronts everywhere, we can understand that we live in a sort of buyers' market in retail space. Giants such as Thor Equities are selling off most of their retail portfolio.

Is that bad news? Quite the contrary. Let me give you a piece of advice, as a professional who has seen many market cycles. If you're a buyer and interested in the retail sector - now is a good time to buy property. If you want to succeed in real estate, you must see past the current market situation. Things change, and the market follows a slightly random, but overall clearly recognizable curve. Of course, there are certain types of businesses that can benefit from the increased inventory and lower prices of former retail locations: anything related to healthcare, veterinarian clinics, gyms, and day spas, for example.

Now, let's discuss a type of commercial real estate that has natural appeal to practically every investor, for the simple reason that in order to be happy and exist in this world, we all must eat something - and celebrate life - every now and then.

Restaurants

I'd like to start this section with a little background story about me that I rather enjoy telling over a couple of drinks.

Throughout the 1990s, Mayor Rudy Giuliani waged a war against pornography in New York City. Rudy fought against strip clubs, porn theaters, and so on. Not that I have anything against that industry, per se, but I'd be the first to say New York used to have a bit too much of it, and it served as a hotbed for organized crime, the drug trade, and corruption. To make a long story short, the mayor succeeded rather spectacularly in kicking all these "undesirable" elements from around 42nd Street, Times Square and a bunch of places Downtown. An impressive mass of ground-level real estate properties lost their pornographically inclined tenants and became available for rent. One of those properties was a spacious former adult movie theater at 28 7th Avenue South, in Greenwich Village.

As a young, hungry investor I managed to arrange a deal that allowed me to become the proud owner of a former porno theater in downtown Manhattan. I took over that establishment and turned it into an upscale, successful restaurant. It took me exactly a year to have the place rebuilt and to get all the permits. The restaurant opened in 1997, and stayed in business until 2003.

This wasn't the first business that I owned. At the time, I was already a well-established broker and investor. Since my first days in America I promised myself that whatever happened, I'd always think like an entrepreneur and act like one. By and large, I've kept that promise. Before I opened my Village restaurant, I owned a successful moving company - and an employment agency before that. And earlier in Italy, I did well financially and had a lot of fun buying and selling cool export items and exotic seafood in the famous Venetian market, *Marcati di Realto*, at Campo della Pescaria.

But back to that restaurant. I was excited to own the place. It was my baby. Today owning a restaurant probably wouldn't be as interesting to me. I'm much more interested in angel investing, and I have plenty on my plate, pun intended. Back then though, I found the restaurant business very interesting. So, for a while, I ran two businesses in downtown Manhattan at the same time: a real estate brokerage and a restaurant.

Owning a restaurant can be a fun if challenging business. It takes a special disposition to be involved in a restaurant business and you have to try it out to find out if you fall into that category. To be profitable, a restaurant needs a liquor license. You a must share the menu with the community board and get it approved.

A restaurant that serves liquor may theoretically stay open until 4 A.M. in the United States, but in practice most of the community boards would want to limit those hours, especially such tough community boards as the ones in Greenwich Village or the East Village. Don't be surprised, don't be taken aback - it's just part of doing business in the city.

A word of wisdom from a battle-tested restaurateur-turned-realtor: if you can, you should buy the property where your restaurant is located. The restaurant business is always in a state of flux, and owning the property offers a great backup for the restaurant: you can use your equity to support the restaurant through market fluctuations.

Back when I did own the restaurant, I had the option to buy the building within first 18 months of the lease, but after I finished building the place, I had no money left to put down. By the time I'd saved enough and came to my landlord to buy the building, the opportunity was gone. I was late to exercise the purchase option by six months, so my landlord doubled the asking price for. There's a Russian expression "to bite one's elbows", which means roughly the same as "to cry over spilled milk." Man, I've been biting my elbows for a long time for letting that deal slip away. Learn from my mistakes!

Overall, the restaurant business was good to me. During my tenure as a restaurateur I met a beautiful bartender who later became my wife, and today we have two beautiful kids.

Hotels

I've said it already, but it's worth repeating: today the hotel business in NYC is prospering like never before. Manhattan has over 1,000 hotels, and at the time of this writing, 92 new hotels with a mind-boggling 15,649 rooms are being constructed.

To give you better understanding of the opportunities you may encounter in the hotel real estate niche, I should talk briefly about M-zoning.

M stands for Manufacturing.

- M1 zone is designated for light manufacturing;
- M2 is assigned to warehouses;
- M3 means heavy industrial.

Hotels nowadays step more and more confidently into M zones in NYC, but there's a very clear distinction here from the hotelier's point of view. Even though M1 is within "the same letter" with M2 and M3, there's little in common between the M1 zone and the other two. You can develop hotels in an M1 zone, but not in M2 and M3—unless you're prepared to wait 1.5 years for a special permit, which you may or may not receive.

That's almost common knowledge nowadays, but what fewer people know is that you can actually build a hotel or convert another type of building into a hotel in an R-zone. R stands for "residential".

C-Zone is "fair game" for any hotel developer: you can have a hotel practically anywhere within C-Zone. You may have guessed that C stands for "commercial".

Over the last few years, we've observed a very interesting phenomenon that became possible thanks to the banks.

Increasingly, real estate developers started building mixed use hotel/condominium buildings. An example of such a development is the Hayat-Andaz hotel at 75 Wall Street. From the ground to the 17th floor it's a hotel, while floors 18 to 40 include approximately 170 condos. The W Hotel at 123 Washington Street in Manhattan offers hotel rooms on floors from 1 to 26, followed by large furnished suites up to the 32nd floor, and finally residential luxury condos all the way up to the 57th floor of the building. Another great development is the Four Seasons Residences at 30 Park Place, a five-star hotel in the lower forty floors, with forty more floors of luxury condominiums.

There's a reason for this trend. As I wrote in the beginning of this book, real estate is built by banks. Today, banks are choosing to diversify their risk and invest in more than one type of property, even when they invest in a single building. That's why they're more eager to provide money for mixed hotel/residential developments.

When it comes to mixed-use buildings, a developer may have a special interest in selling all his or her condos, while preferring to keep the hotel component. That's what happened to a very successful building on Billionaires Row. The hotel management company, Park Hyatt, was bound by a long-term agreement with Donald Trump not to open another hotel under this brand in the area. But the moment the agreement expired, they immediately signed a contract with Extell's Gary Barnett, and he built Park Hyatt at 153 West 57th Street. Gary Barnett is an experienced owner and developer who usually builds condos. In this building, the first 27 floors are occupied by the hotel, restaurant and spa, and the developer was interested in keeping the hotel in order to compete against the Four Seasons and Mandarin Oriental. But eventually he changed his mind and sold the hotel part of the building to a Chinese investor for $300 million.

A peculiar slice of hotel business is the time share. In Manhattan, you can only find precious few time share hotels. One notable *former* example is The Dominic Hotel in SoHo (previously known as the Trump Hotel SoHo). Until recently you could buy a three-month time share in that hotel and become a business partner with Donald Trump and his hotel management company. As of today, Mr. Trump has moved on from managing that hotel to what seems like bigger and better things, and the hotel changed its name and its business model.

Other current examples include The Manhattan Club at 200 West 56th Street, The Phillips Club on 155 West 66th Street, The Hilton Club at 1335 Avenue of The Americas, and the St. Regis Residence Club at 2 East 55th Street.

I've said it once, and it's worth repeating: we live in the epoch of massive disruption in commercial real estate. We saw how WeWork uprooted the traditional office real estate model, and we witnessed Amazon pulling the rug from under brick and mortar retail. Something similar nearly happened with Airbnb and the hotel industry, though not as smoothly, and not quite as legally.

Most people today know what Airbnb is and what it does. It allows internet users the opportunity to rent apartments or houses on a budget in almost any country and city in the world. If you don't mind playing host to people you've never met, you can list your residence on Airbnb, earn a little extra cash, and become a "crowdsourced hotelier".

The problem is that this is referred to as "short-term leasing", and it's - gasp! - illegal in the state of New York. The city has created a special law that requires all rental agreements to be 30 days or longer. If you want to operate a hotel in NY, that's fine, too. You'll have to pay a rather substantial hotel tax, but you can also collect tax from your guests. You must file a Certificate of Registration application with the Department of Finance and obtain a Certificate of Authority, and so on.

Airbnb tried to get away with not doing any of that, and attempted to snatch away a solid chunk of the city's hotel business. None too happy about this, New York State Attorney General Eric T. Schneiderman immediately subpoenaed Airbnb's business documentation and shortly thereafter published a report outlining the "widespread illegality across New York City listings on the Airbnb website." As a result, over 5,000 property owners and aspiring hoteliers incurred substantial fines from the state. A bit of a fiasco for Airbnb, and a small but important win for New York's hotel industry.

Today you can still rent a house in NYC via Airbnb, but it would have to be for 30 days or longer.

No offence to Airbnb, but I find this fair. Do you know what it takes to develop a hotel - any hotel - in our city? The average construction cost for a hotel in Manhattan is $354 per square foot. By comparison, in the notoriously more expensive city of Zurich, Switzerland, developing a hotel costs only $328 per square foot.

Yes, the hotel business in New York City is challenging, and so is, by association, the hotel real estate business. And yet, the hotel market in the city continues to be attractive to developers. That's because along with the huge costs and risks that come with building, owning, or managing a hotel in the city, there also comes great profit.

The question becomes whether or not you have what it takes for such an endeavor. Developing a hotel in New York City is a massive undertaking, not for the faint of heart. But I'll show you the ropes, and you decide what you want to do afterwards.

Essentially, you have two options: you can either do a ground-up development, or convert an existing building into a hotel. Today you will find a slew of various hotel franchises, such as Days Inn, Holiday Inn, Hampton Inn, Marriott Courtyard, Radisson - any of them will be very pleased to gain a new entry into NYC's market.

Or you can open your own independent boutique hotel brand, which is something we often see. NYC has many single-hotel brands with no presence anywhere else in the world, all individual, and usually catering to VIP guests.

If you're an entrepreneur with a solid vision and adequate financial standing, you can always find equity partners interested in the hotel business, and there will always be banks eager to finance hotel development in Manhattan. There are hedge funds that will give you equity, and even cash as the down-payment for your new hotel! Also, you can always find developers with development sites ready and waiting for you. It's like shooting fish in a barrel... if you know what you're doing.

But really, things are looking up for the hotel business in New York City, so chances are you're probably going to be successful. The tourist business in the city has been booming for decades, and is constantly on the rise. This boom manifests itself in a number of interesting ways.

For example, just a few days ago, the New York City Council announced that Manhattan has too many tourist buses! Too many, mind you, not because they are going around empty. On the contrary, these buses are always full. Rather there are too many of them because they've begun to dangerously clog regular Manhattan traffic and cause accidents. According to this report, the number of tour buses in the city grew from 54 in 2003 to 237 in 2016!

New Broadway shows, new cultural hubs - even entire new neighborhoods to rival the old Manhattan attractions - all ensure continuous future growth for the city. To guarantee the growth of tourism, the city needs something known as "throughput": a steady flow of tourists in and out. To that end, Manhattan makes it easier for tourists to proceed to their next destination and then come back to the city again! More and more cruise ships leave Manhattan for a brief Caribbean cruise (so that a new batch of tourists can come to the city in the meantime), and then return back to Big Apple, where the same tourists can pour even more cash into the city's economy... and its hotels.

Now that we've covered hotel real estate in some detail, let's move on to the next logical type of commercial property. It's just like a hotel - but for your car.

Garages

A few days ago, I was invited to an event where I was supposed to be honored among a group of ten prominent Manhattan real estate brokers and educators for my involvement with an important New York real estate organization: the New York City Residential Specialist Professional Program, organized by Real Estate Board of New York. I was naïve enough to decide to travel to the event in a nice Mercedes, and arrive in style fifteen minutes ahead of time. If you know Manhattan, you're probably already smiling. You guessed it. I drove around looking for a parking spot- but I never found one. I ended up spending a small fortune in a nearby garage for just a couple of hours of parking time. I was late and missed all the best hors d'oeuvres!

My point is that the garage business in New York City is damn profitable! And with car manufacturers ramping up production year after year, garages in Manhattan can only increase in demand - and in price.

There are some interesting trends in New York City. One of the recent ones, when it comes to garages, actually manifested itself in cutting down on large open-air parking places. This makes sense. Remember the notion of "highest and best use"? Well, convenient as it may be to have a large open-air parking area, a landowner will probably make more money by selling the lot, and a developer would be economically correct to build a high-rise residential or commercial building on it. This also makes sense from the point of view of the garage business. Having a multi-story garage in the basement of the new building is more beneficial to car owners and garage owners alike.

Owning a garage is a cash business - a *great* cash business. Garages in Manhattan make serious money on monthly memberships for regular cars and SUV's, as well as on motorcycle parking, especially seasonally.

Which reminds me. Want to join me and my guys on our planned "NYC - LA - Vegas - NYC" Harley run? Give me a buzz, and we can talk about it.

Even better than a monthly membership, those garages that offer daily and hourly parking make most of the money (from the likes of me, when I get so carried away with my professional achievements that I briefly forget in which city I live and drive).

There are a few major garage operators in the city, such as Enterprise Parking and Icon Parking. These businesses have a great market share. However, small independent parking garages are always successful, and are always on the lookout for new garages and new locations.

When you're in charge of a new real estate development, you always face the parking requirement. Depending on zoning, you have to create a certain number of parking spots. So, if your business situation allows, I implore you to consider including a garage in whatever you're developing. Once you complete the project, you can either become a garage operator or sell your new parking spots. That really depends on your goals, but either way, you will earn a lot.

Conversions

What I'm about to tell you now will sound a bit philosophical at first, but bear with me. This is actually the most valuable and practical part of this chapter.

What's single most important mental skill essential for major success in real estate? I would say, hands down, **flexibility.**

If you have the ability to be flexible (either innate or developed), you'll see wide-open doors where other people see impenetrable concrete walls. Whenever I reveal real estate secrets to people, very often their reaction is: wow, this is so obvious! Why didn't I think of this? Well, sometimes things are so obvious that they hide in plain sight (like in that old Edgar Poe story about the purloined letter).

One obvious secret is that real estate is fluid. Buildings appear solid and permanent, but that permanence is an illusion. That's why no one can count the exact number of buildings in Manhattan. Every day some old buildings magically disappear, while others begin construction, and so it will always be.

But what is also fluid (and where you as a real estate investor can reap great benefits simply by being flexible) is how buildings are *used*.

In older Manhattan neighborhoods, as well as in some very populated younger ones, for many years we've seen high prices for retail and office spaces. However, banks rule this world, and lately they found great advantage in underwriting decisions based on the highest value to be gained from the residential use of real estate. As soon as a bank begins to suspect that a certain commercial building containing a store or an office might be more profitable as a residential condominium - you can bet it will be converted to residential use in a hurry!

That's what usually happens during a residential boom. However, as soon as the residential market becomes saturated or slightly over-used, the response by banks is samurai-style swift (and merciless)! Suddenly, rather than being converted to condominiums, we witness old commercial buildings being turned into hotels. This is a trend today, due to the massive growth in tourism.

Similarly, in the recent past, when hotels became somewhat less profitable, all of a sudden, we saw a wave of conversions from hotels to residential use. A great example of the latter is the purchase of The Plaza by Elad Group back in mid 1990s, and the conversion of this famous 110-year-old New York landmark into condominiums. As of today, only about a half of Plaza Hotel is still a hotel... but things may change, as The Plaza is for sale once again, by its current co-owners, an Indian corporation with rather non-Indian sounding name Sahara Group (75% stakes) and Prince Al-Waleed bin Talal of Saudi Arabia, jointly with Ashkenazy Acquisition Corporation of New York (25% stake). I predict it will remain a mixed-use building, but I wouldn't be surprised by some interesting new variations in how it's managed.

Probably the most representative example of flexibility in real estate is the principle of **adaptive reuse**, which took decades to formulate and put into practice, and which was initially met with perplexed attitude and resistance.

Adaptive reuse is the approach that involves maintaining or restoring a historic building (or, in some cases, a historic architectural or civil engineering structure)—and finding a new use for it, in many cases so wildly different from what was originally intended that the architect or the original owner would be the first to be taken aback.

The already familiar High Line, formerly an abandoned and partially dismantled railroad track, and now a successful park, serves as the perfect example of adaptive reuse. But there are countless others across Manhattan. Another example includes "Old Jeff", aka The Jefferson Market Courthouse, the iconic Victorian-style building designed by Frederick Clarke Withers and Calvert Vaux on the corner of 6th avenue and West 10th street, now hosts a branch of New York Public Library. Or the Park Avenue Armory—formerly a mix of a military facility and social club for scions of the city's most prominent families— which currently serves as a cultural venue hosting concerts and art exhibitions.

The takeaway here is that whichever type of real estate you invest in, you should remain flexible and keep your options open for alternative ways of using it. The difference between a flexible and rigid mindset may be counted in the millions.

Own Your Business Property!

When you deal with retail or office space, the best way to be successful is buying property for a ready tenant. That's how Donald Trump's commercial real estate partner, Sam Sutton, became wildly successful. His main business model is securing the anchor tenant - and only then does he begin to look for a building. If not the tenant, at the very least you must have a vision, a clear and profitable concept for the use of your property. If you have a tenant or a concept you will be successful.

I may have said this once or twice already, but just like with residential properties, when it comes to your business space, I recommend that you own it. In fact, I don't see any redeeming quality in renting! If you can afford the rent, it means you can afford buying that property, and your mortgage payment wouldn't be significantly higher than your rent. Then should your business turn a little worse for whatever reason, you can offset your downturns with your equity. This way, rather than burning through your money during more difficult times, you will make your building work for you.

Successful businesses that buy their buildings - no matter how expensive they may be - never regret it, and they often become even more successful if they decide to resell their real estate property during a high market.

And this brings us to the next segment of our chapter on commercial real estate.

Leaseback

Leaseback, also known as "sale-and-lease-back" is a very interesting property management technique, usually applied by entrepreneurs who own their business space but need extra capital for expanding or promoting their business. To acquire the necessary cash, they sell their building and then - you guessed it! - lease it back from the new owner for 5, 10, or more years.

For instance, suppose Tom owns a pharmacy store and a building that contains it. Tom doesn't need the building, but what he does need is capital to expand his business and open a few more locations. Tom sells his building to Rachel, but remains in it as a tenant. Rachel now becomes Tom's landlord and receives rent from Tom every month. Tom, however, receives a multimillion-dollar sum from Rachel on the closing, and if he invests that money well and grows his business, at some point in the future he may even be able to buy that building back from Rachel!

That was an abstract, hypothetical example just to illustrate the concept. As for real life, the hottest sale-and-lease-back opportunity in New York currently is the $500 million deal on Sotheby's iconic 500,000 square feet headquarters at 1334 York Avenue (between East 71st and East 72nd streets). The building has 10 floors, roughly 50,000 square feet each, and some of its ceilings are 24 feet high. Sotheby's announced its *most recent* decision to sell and lease back the building several years ago, in 2013, and had been casually shopping for a buyer ever since. I emphasized the "most recent" decision to sell and lease back because the famous auction house actually has a peculiar history of leasing that building, buying it, and selling and leasing it back again, and after a $150 million renovation by Kohn Pedersen Fox in 2003, buying it again! This time around though, the announced lease back is going to be short-term, until Sotheby's finds a new location for its headquarters... unless they change their mind and buy the building back again.

Any sell-and-lease-back deal is appealing for investors and new commercial landlords. You can get a property *and* a tenant who's already settled in that property. There's no need to rebuild or reconstruct anything, and you don't have to provide such extra incentives as free tenancy—which in commercial buildings can take up to six months when a *new* tenant moves in. Here you have a tenant who's paying rent from day one, and you can always get a security deposit, and successful businesses can give you the equivalent of 6 to 12-months of rent as a security deposit. I very much recommend that you do obtain such a security deposit. If later on you decide to sell that building, having the security deposit gives you extra ammunition for negotiations because you have enough time to find a new tenant, and that time is guaranteed by the security deposit placed in your escrow account.

I must mention that in New York you're not obligated to place the security deposit into an escrow account if your tenant doesn't request it. One way or another, if your tenant is not a major national or publicly-traded company, but for example a small retailer with a small margin of safety, I'd advise that you get at least 6, or preferably 12 months' worth of rent. This way you can sleep better because the security deposit gives you the safety cushion to find a new tenant.

Ground Leases

This chapter on commercial real estate wouldn't be complete if I didn't mention ground leases. A ground lease can be defined as a long-term net lease (usually 49 years or 99 years) of land, including any improvements on it. You can ground-lease a vacant lot of land, or an office building, or a large residential/mixed use building.

Ground leases offer multiple advantages to landowners and tenants alike.

If you're a tenant, taking a ground lease allows you to secure the property for the duration of your lifetime - without the need for a down payment, which would be required if you were to purchase that property. You can ground-lease some properties that wouldn't be available for sale because in some cases the property owner may be unwilling to part with his possession, but would be quite okay leasing it and turning it into a permanent source of passive income. You can get a mortgage for a ground lease, but the financing you obtain will not be granted against the leased asset. This means that should worse come to worst, and your business turns out to be not quite the success you expected, the bank won't take away your business location and you won't lose everything you invested in it.

If you're a landlord, the advantages of ground leases will be even more apparent. In fact, a ground lease is one of the most interesting and lucrative ways to bank on a real estate investment, so I'd like you to seriously consider this option. If you ground-lease your property, you won't have to pay any capital gain taxes, and, in most cases, you probably won't have to pay property transfer tax either. The tenant will be responsible for management, maintenance and improvement of your property - and will bear all costs. The property will therefore generate easy and hassle-free passive income for many decades and even generations to come, while remaining within your family. You can mortgage the property and refinance it - and after the lease term has finished, your heir will get the property back with all the improvements made by the tenant!

Do you see how important it is to know these little techniques and professional secrets?

A Few Examples

Throughout my real estate career, I've taken part in commercial real estate deals that have been beneficial to both sellers and buyers.

As an example, a 17-story office building in which I was based and which I also managed for the owner, had been bought for $11 million in 2001. By 2004, it was converted into a residential property and sold by the developer for $70 million. What's curious is that the developer sold floors 2 through 17, but kept the retail space on the ground floor. He refinanced, and took an $8.5 million mortgage. Then a few years later, the owner decided to leave the retail part of it, and sold just that one floor for $20 million.

Sometime later, during a different transaction, I worked another owner to sell an office building on Broadway near Maiden Lane to a developer for $50 million. That building was later converted into a Marriott hotel by a sponsor. However, the basement, first, and second floor of the building had been converted into a retail space, which was sold to Gap one and a half years ago for $70 million! As a result, the top floors - 3 to 9—ended up costing the developer practically nothing! Today it's a hotel of 150 rooms and suites, which brings in over$5 million yearly of profit.

One of my clients - an investor - was interested in a certain retail space available for sale, and had $6 million to invest in it. Unfortunately, the seller wanted to sell it together with another retail space in the corner of the same building for the total amount of $14 million. My client didn't like that corner very much, and didn't have the extra $8 million, but the seller was adamant about not selling just one retail space. I helped the client formulate the creative approach to the problem. We surprised the seller with our counteroffer: to sell us not a corner retail space, and not the originally planned retail space, but the available space between the two, which the owner didn't originally plan to sell. We succeeded in buying it, and my client ended up owning an office occupied by a major bank, which had a 15-year rental agreement. The bank also happened to have a so-called **triple net lease**. It's a useful term to remember - be on the lookout for the triple net lease deals. A triple net lease in commercial real estate means that the tenant is responsible for everything related to maintenance of the rental property, and the landlord is only responsible for repairing the major structural defects of the building. Retail and office condos are known as NN net lease. It's when property owner pays common charges and real estate taxes and tenants pays rent. That commercial condominium had no structural defects, so my client didn't have to worry much about being involved in any repair work. Two years later the client sold the same office space for $9 million - and then a few years later, the new owner sold it again for $14 million. (That's the fabled Elliot Bogod's Golden Touch™ in action.)

Having been a broker in Manhattan for over two decades, I've helped arrange virtually every type of complex transaction possible: multi-party sells, or refinancing on joint ventures when one or more of the partners want to sell a property mid-development and others want to remain in the project, and so on. Since I know many landlords and developers, this gives me considerable insider advantage. This proverbial "Rolodex" allows me to connect links of the real estate chain together and structure some interesting and profitable deals.

As a broker, I can tell you it's never easy to construct a joint venture in real estate. But in my experience, any well-organized joint venture is worth the trouble. Partners whose combined areas of expertise complement each other inevitably become successful, and in some of the best cases a joint venture can grow into a long-term business relationship.

CHAPTER VI: THE REAL ESTATE INVESTOR TOOLKIT

Have you been on a moving walkway in an airport or another similar public place? Know the ones I'm talking about? All you need is to step on it and it will carry you forward all by itself?

Well, real estate investing is a bit like that, too. All you need is to take the first step in the right direction and it will propel you forward toward success. Of course, you can continue walking even while on the moving walkway and that will get you to your goal sooner. Knowing a few tricks of the trade can help.

Let's begin with the most important one.

Earn as you Buy, or The Secret of Success

Wait, what? Earn as you buy?

Yes. In a nutshell, that magic formula contains everything you need to know in order to succeed in real estate investing.

Real estate is strategic, much like chess. You'll earn money when you sell the property you're about to buy - maybe years or even decades from today. You will also create passive income when you bring tenants into your property. The equity of your property is a key factor, and it has a precise monetary equivalent. There are also a few other ways to generate cash from your real estate property - which I'll describe to you in this chapter.

On the other hand, you shouldn't under any circumstances be oblivious of the amount of tax you'll pay for your property— including the tax on any profit you make from it.

First and foremost, you must understand that the success of your investment depends on how you choose the property to buy, how you buy it, and what you think about when you are choosing and buying it.

Let's talk about choosing what you buy. We already discussed in some detail the "co-op vs condo" (non-)dilemma and then reviewed the styles and advantages of Manhattan townhouses. Suppose we agree that buying a condo in one of Manhattan's thousands of multi-unit buildings is the way to go.

Which building should you choose?

As is often the case, that choice would very much depend on your individual preferences, but let me first give you the lay of the land.

In simple terms, residential buildings in Manhattan can be categorized by age or by service. These categories overlap: the newest buildings tend to have maximum service.

Age-wise, buildings can be roughly distinguished as "pre-war" (built before WWII), "post-war" (everything between 1945 and 2000), and "new" (erected between 2000 and today).

Pre-war buildings are mostly co-ops and rentals, even though exceptions abound. They often feature high ceilings and fairly soundproof walls between the units. On the flip side, the plumbing may not be the most robust, and therefore you're not likely to find many pre-war buildings allowing a washer and drier in the unit.

Post-war buildings tend to be somewhat generic in design. The noise level might be slightly more noticeable than in a pre-war building, and the ceilings may be, should I just say, comparable to those in the houses designed by the great American architect Frank Lloyd Wright, who was known for calculating what he envisioned as the "optimal" ceiling heights based on his own, rather short, stature. However, these buildings are often in the "goldilocks zone" from the price perspective—meaning they are usually more affordable than both pre-war and new constructions, their elevators are more spacious, and their windows larger than in older buildings, letting in more light. Post-war buildings typically include such amenities as a laundry room and a gym.

Buildings of the new era make me optimistic about New York City's future and that of humankind in general. Spectacular design, lavish amenities, and spacious, airy apartments with huge ceilings - everything in these new buildings signifies the arrival of the Platinum Era of our city. Of course, all that precious metal comes with the appropriately high price tag, but if the ultimate in luxury real estate is what you're after, then the new construction building is what you should aim for.

In terms of services, Manhattan buildings range from no-service to full-service. Understanding the sometimes-fuzzy terminology that describes the types of available services should help you navigate these murky waters.

"Full-service" means just what it sounds like: 24-7 porters, doormen, concierges, and maids, as well as a live-in manager and engineering team. Even though all the people on staff are paid moderately large salaries, full service is often provided in buildings with a huge number of apartments, so the additional cost is spread across a lot of real estate owners. Traditionally you'll be expected to tip staff for their services, which can run up to a couple of thousand dollars per year, but if you can afford buying an apartment in a full-service building, the tips probably won't break you. Residents put tips in envelopes also containing seasonal greeting cards, and personally hand them to every member of the building staff - which is a great opportunity to meet, greet, and express appreciation to people who work very hard to make *your* life more comfortable.

Is there fuller-than-full service, you may ask?

Actually, there is. In so-called "white-glove" buildings, you will get full service, and it will be on the level comparable to those of the world's best 5-star hotels. Your pet hamster will be provided with a 24-7 personal assistant. (I'm almost not joking.)

A "doorman" building is a step down, and in practice this can range from 24-7 rotating security team and a live-in super, to an 8-hours-a day doorman, too busy preparing to his college exam to pay attention to what's going in the building, and no super. The prices will vary correspondingly.

An "elevator" building may or may not have a live-in super, but it definitely won't have a doorman. Some of these buildings have freight elevators in addition to a regular one—in which case it may include a part-time handyman and possibly a part-time cleaner from once a week to once a month. Some of the elevator buildings include modern "electronic doorman" systems, which offer security and safety for any packages delivered to you, while also saving money on staff salaries. A few elevator buildings in Manhattan still have the old-school elevators operated by a uniformed elevator attendant. Living in such a building will make you feel like a character from *Mad Men*...or like you're paying extra for something you could do perfectly well by yourself.

And finally, a "walk-up" building. This one probably won't have an elevator. Or a full-time super. The condos, however, will cost much less. Worth considering just for that reason.

But let me say something slightly counter-intuitive: if you can afford paying a higher price for a piece of property, you probably should. Why? Because the price you paid today will multiply by the time you're ready to sell this piece of property. "Earn as you buy" - remember?

The price that you pay for your property today is of utmost importance. It's as General Maximus said in the beginning of the movie *Gladiator*: "What we do in life, echoes in Eternity". If it was true back during the Roman Empire, then it's even more so in today's information age. As soon as the deal is closed, the information about the price you paid for your property becomes immediately available via computer to bank appraisers, and that information will remain online forever, affecting the future fate of the property and your ability to sell it. That's why it's so important to buy your property for the right price. Which doesn't always mean "the lowest price"!

Your mastery of price negotiation, and your ability to find a mutually beneficial compromise and see the "big picture" while negotiating the price are crucial because they will influence the quality of the deal and the speed with which you can win that purchase.

It's common today that a seller, not knowing you, would request a POF (Proof of Funds). This could be a letter from your bank, or your recent bank statement; a letter from your lender who can provide money for a down payment; the proof of the actual down payment, and so on.

Only after you've provided all these necessary confirmations and assurances will your seller agree to task their lawyer with preparing the contract, which will then be sent to your lawyer. One of the fundamental psychological "secrets" of negotiating a deal is that you should make your seller feel as safe and comfortable as possible when the seller is dealing with you.

Make it easy to trust you by being open, transparent, and obliging with any necessary information - and you can win "points" with the seller, which you can then turn to your advantage. If that's how you make it work, you can be sure that the contract will be sent within the shortest possible time, and the deal will go smoothly.

In today's market, we are witnessing a dramatic difference between what sellers expect to get for their property and what buyers are prepared to pay. Buyers always seem to think they can get the kind of price the seller would never agree on, and vice versa. It's always been like that, but my observation confirms that the chasm is continuously increasing, especially in Manhattan.

To make the deal happen, we must find a consensus between the buyer and the seller, the common ground between these two opposite, conflicting interests. It's my job as a real estate broker to bridge the gap between mutually conflicting expectations, to bring both the buyers and the sellers "back to Earth", so to speak, and make the deal a reality.

The alternative is unpleasant and unproductive. A lowball offer - no matter how much a buyer may think that offer is fair - is a surefire way to instantly eliminate the seller's desire to continue any dialogue. The seller may never come back to that buyer at all. In today's market in Manhattan, the technique of "lowball first and raise the offer later" just doesn't work.

However, if the buyer patiently and repeatedly makes moderate, reasonable offers to multiple sellers - then at some point, sooner or later, one of the buyers will accept the offer. That's why I always recommend to my buyer clients not to fall in love with a property and not to keep raising the price. Just wait until you find the optimal price for the optimal property, and then be ready to "pull the trigger".

Every purchase you make must be strategic. It must have an exact numeric goal. You must plan how much you will earn from it. And you shouldn't take that figure out of thin air. You must know exactly how much money you're spending when you're buying a piece of real estate property. And you should only commit to the purchase when a figure based on iron-clad data satisfies you. Otherwise, leave the deal. Walk away. It's OK to walk away even from the title closing, even if you were already holding a pen to the paper. I've done it more than once when something about the deal at the very last moment suddenly raised a red flag.

You have to be ready to walk away. Trust me, it's worth it.

There are exceptions. If what you are buying has no monetary equivalent, but you know with complete certainty that you are investing in happiness, health, or safety (yours or people you love) - by all means, buy it, as long as it doesn't come with a cost that might negatively affect the happiness, health or safety of these parties at a later time.

Making these decisions can be incredibly challenging. What helps untie the knot between "pro" and "con" is information, because it's information that allows you to be strategic about everything you do in the first place.

The Value of Information

The great financier J.P. Morgan was a figure of legendary proportions. He made his fortune in commodities: pork bellies, orange juice, barley, cocoa, corn, cotton, and so on. He amassed such a huge fortune that the entire astronomical cost of the Metropolitan Museum collection today is smaller than the amount of money J.P. Morgan donated to the museum (adjusted for inflation). As if by gift of prophetic vision, J.P. Morgan knew exactly which commodity would be abundant and which would be scarce, which prices would go up or down – and he never made a mistake predicting the market. Not once.

According to one of the legends surrounding the life of the great financier, the mystery of J.P. Morgan's extraordinary foresight had a simple secret behind it. The way the story has it, even before he amassed his extraordinary fortune, J.P. Morgan was well-off: enough to be able to invest in a penthouse at the top floor of one of the tallest skyscrapers of the time, at 14 Wall Street. The top of that building was designed with the following architectural design challenge by the firm of architects Trowbridge & Livingston: "what if we place the Mausoleum of Halicarnassus on top of St Mark's Campanile?"

So (says the legend), J.P. Morgan bought the penthouse and lived and worked in the Manhattan version of the Mausoleum. The view from his home office must have been magnificent. J.P. Morgan could see all of Manhattan and the New York Harbor from his window. He enjoyed the view of the harbor so much that he installed a telescope in his office window to see even better. Watching the harbor through that telescope during his leisure time, J.P. Morgan saw every ship that entered the harbor and figured out which commodities were transported to the city. His success was, in fact, virtually risk-free, and his ability to collect ridiculously high dividends, understandable.

The yarn I just presented to you was passed among business people (including real estate brokers) for many generations – and even used in marketing campaigns. But, alas, it's a work of fiction! J.P.Morgan passed away in 1913, merely a year after the building on 14 Wall Street had been completed – and even though the financier indeed owned the apartment on 31st floor, unfortunately, he didn't live long enough to enjoy the views.

The moral of this story, however, is true. Scientia potentia est: knowledge is power.

This was true during the times of Imam Ali, Thomas Hobbes and Sir Francis Bacon-all variously credited with the authorship of this aphorism. And today, it's even truer. As a real estate broker and advisor to hundreds of real estate investors, I place tremendous value on my ability to have real-time access to high-quality information and my ability to interpret that information correctly – and so should you.

Having the correct information and knowing what it means, you can make the right purchase, the right investment for yourself, your co-investors, and your clients.

The next question: how do you find that information?

Let me ask you this: can you name the single most fundamental method for obtaining information, the one children learn to use starting around the age of two?

That's right. To obtain information, you ask questions. And after you get the answers, you question and cross-check them.

What questions should you ask?

By now you can probably guess my usual response. It depends on each unique situation and your individual preferences. However, there are certain basic principles behind the art of asking questions in real estate. Create the list of all things you wouldn't want to discover about your new apartment on the morning after you moved in and be sure to ask questions about every single one.

For example, if I were shopping for an apartment for myself and my family right now, here's what I'd ask, and why.

- Are there any smokers leaving in the nearby apartments, on the same floor, or on the nearest floors above and below? (I hate nicotine, and I sure as hell wouldn't want my kids to be exposed to any second-hand smoke. Imagine if I spent a ton of money only to find out the next morning that I'm besieged by smokers?!)
- Are all the listed amenities included in the common charges? Do some and/or all of them come for an extra charge, and if so, how much do these costs amount to? I enjoy staying in shape, and so does every member of my family. While we do get solid workouts outside of our house, we also value the private gym and swimming pool in the building.
- If there's no washer and drier already installed, will they be allowed? (Actually, I probably wouldn't even bother to look at an apartment without a washer and drier. As far as kids go, mine are very neat, but still they're kids, you know...)
- What are the current (and future) neighbors like? (I wouldn't want to discover that one of my neighbors is a drug addict or, for example, a hoarder with a habit of bringing home every piece of discarded furniture he sees out in the street...bed bugs and all. Urgh!)

You should ask what's important to you. Don't be modest and don't skip any questions.

Also don't rely on the most obvious "biological" source of information: your senses. When you visit an apartment for sale, look, listen, touch, smell - and taste (the quality of food in neighborhood restaurants will be important to you).

For example, you may come across a two-bedroom apartment in which one of the bedrooms is a cozy room, large enough for a queen-size bed, a dresser and some walkway space, and conveniently dark because it doesn't have any windows. Guess what, that's not a two-bedroom apartment because the room with no windows is not a bedroom: it's a "den", or a "home office". That apartment should cost significantly less than an actual two-bedroom apartment.

Or suppose there's a window, or several windows, but they open onto a construction site. This may be a sign that in the near future all these windows will have to be bricked up (these are called "lot line windows," also colloquially known as "illegal windows"). If you have them, be ready for some fun: the bricklayers will spend a day or two in the apartment you bought and fill your windows shut. Wait, it gets better. You'll be the one obligated to pay them for this!

When you're in the apartment - do you sense vibrations from the building equipment or the street below? Do you hear noises from the elevator lobby, neighboring apartments, or from the street? Do you smell gas fumes rising from the underground garage? Is one of the walls of the apartment oddly warm because of the boiler right behind it?

One family I was showing condos to repeatedly slammed the apartment doors, listening to the noise. I praised them for their attention to detail. Of course, it's vital for your well-being to know that if a tired neighbor shows up in three in the morning and shuts their door too vigorously, they won't wake up your entire household! Another family flushed the toiled and listened from behind the closed door - for similar reasons.

Be scientific about it: when it comes to knowledge, nothing beats hard evidence.

Suppose you buy an apartment, and a current owner tells you that the unit they are offering to sell represents 1,000 square feet of space. How do you assess the validity of that information? Do you take the seller's word for it? (I'll give you a hint: no.) Do you go online to some specialized portal that contains precise information about square footage of every apartment in Manhattan? (Alas, such portal doesn't exist; and even if it existed, the data in it would be hugely inaccurate!)

What you should do is come to the apartment with a ruler and you painstakingly measure it. And that's how you get information you can trust.

I'm going to tell you more about obtaining high-quality information in the chapter on sale cycles - so please read it thoroughly and don't miss any of the important stuff!

But now it would seem appropriate to talk about financing.

Mortgages

We can look at the subject of mortgage from several angles. The very first perspective I'd like you to consider is timing, both for applying and receiving a mortgage. There are two possible scenarios here. You may apply for the mortgage when you already know what property you're going to buy and when you know with a reasonable degree of confidence that your mortgage application will be approved by the bank. In this case, when you make your offer to the seller to buy their property, your offer is characterized as "subject to financing." In the (hopefully unlikely) event that no financial institution agrees to give you the mortgage, you won't be legally obligated to buy the property (there are still a few things to be carefully considered to avoid the highly unpleasant scenario that a seller keeps the property...and your down-payment). This type of offer to buy may be considered a position of certain disadvantage for you as a buyer because the seller may choose another offer over yours - namely, the offer from a buyer who came with check in hand.

However, if you are committed to buying a property, and know the price limit you're comfortable with (plus some reasonable padding), you can apply for a mortgage and get pre-approved by the bank before you even find the right property to buy. In that case, you will be the buyer who makes the offer with check in hand, and you will have the edge over other buyers who have yet to apply for their mortgage and wait for approval. Your offer will be superior to theirs because it's not dependent on mortgage contingency.

The best part is that this strategy will probably allow your broker to negotiate a lower price for the property because the owner will know that the money can be handed to him today - right away, without contingency.

How do you get approved for your mortgage? Let's consider the scenario of buying residential property as one example.

First and foremost, your cost of owning a home <u>must not exceed 40% of your net income</u>.

That's when you buy a condo or a townhouse. When it comes to buying shares in a co-op, the rules are much stricter. Usually it would be expected that your property cost not exceed 30% of your income, and in many cases, especially in some of Manhattan's poshest co-ops, the point is moot because the co-op board will expect you to pay cash!

What is "the cost of owning a home"?

That actually depends of what kind of ownership we're talking about. If you plan to invest in a condominium, the cost is the combination of payments on your debt to the bank, real estate taxes, and the monthly common charges. If you apply for the loan with the goal of purchasing a co-op (in accordance with very strict terminology, that co-op loan is not actually supposed to be referred to as "mortgage," although even professionals call it that for convenience), your cost is comprised only of debt payments and the common charges, taxes not included. If you're requesting a mortgage for a townhouse, or any other kind of single-family property, your cost of ownership includes paying off your debt, real estate taxes, and the cost of obligatory insurance.

When a bank makes these calculations, it also considers any other debts that you may currently have. These debts must not exceed your cost of ownership by more than 10%.

You may want to ask: "Can I borrow enough money from the bank to cover the entire cost of purchasing real estate - or more?"

The answer is no.

Banks want you to be personally invested in your property, rather than just risking money that you borrowed. Your personal interest in the property signifies to the bank that you will not default on your payments and lose the collateral (your new house), having invested your hard-earned money in it. Also, should worse come to worst and you find yourself unable to pay back the loan, the bank would have to foreclose your property, and that costs a lot of money. The legal procedure is expensive; defaults and foreclosures are more likely to happen during a bad economy, which drives real estate prices down and distress sales drop the price additionally. Banks want to make sure that your own money covers the cost of possible foreclosure.

Hence, if you borrow money to buy a condo, banks will typically only give you up to 80% of the price of the property, or up to 90% through "deep leverage", aka "heavy leverage", programs, if you're willing to pay at least a .5% higher interest rate, or if you take out a so-called "dual loan." This means, using my favorite magical word: "equity", that your equity-to-debt ratio when buying a condo can go up to 20/80 or even 10/90 using "deep leverage." With a co-op loan, it would have to be 30/70 (or just 100 equity).

Here's a bit more on deep leverage programs and dual loans. Both of these techniques are meant to give the buyer the badly needed extra percentage in addition to the standard limit of 80% of the property price.

A deep leverage mortgage is comprised of two types of loans: a normal 80% loan and an additional one, of up to 10%. That additional percentage requires the bank to secure the funds by purchasing non-tax-deducible mortgage insurance from an insurance company. As a result, the actual interest rate to the additional percentage may be up to 75% higher! But this 75% is spread evenly over your entire mortgage, resulting in about a 0.5% higher average interest rate.

The dual loan is just what it sounds like. You take out two loans, one for the 80% of the property price, and the other on the remaining 10%. Oddly enough, using this simple approach you would get a lower percentage rate than in the case of the deep leverage mortgage because with the dual loan, the bank is not obligated to pay for the insurance on the extra 10%.

This may seem like the same thing, in essence, but it will cost you less. This is another good example of how knowing small intricate details can save you considerable money.

You can also lower your interest rate if you offer the bank upfront points. Using that strategy, you can win a significant reduction in your interest rate, as each point paid to the bank upfront results in a loan reduction by .25%.

There are a couple of other interesting categories of mortgages that you may find useful to know about.

Interest-only mortgages may be of value to you if your professional occupation involves large bonuses or commissions on major sales. This type of mortgage is structured in such way that every time you pay off a large part of your mortgage in one shot, both the interest rate on your subsequent payment and the monthly amount you must pay become significantly smaller.

Another type of loan, known under its rather complicated name "The 12-month Moving Average Treasury Index Loan", can give you even greater flexibility, allowing you to choose between different payment options every month. Depending on your financial situation that month, you can make a minimum payment, an interest-only payment, or the full monthly payment.

Let's move on now and take a look at mortgages from a different angle.

There are two main types of mortgages: conventional (also known as "conforming") and Jumbo ("nonconforming"). There's also a super-Jumbo, but these are fairly rare.

To understand what these names mean, you should get a basic idea about how the banks make money from real estate loans.

Issuing you a mortgage, a bank makes money twice: from the interest rate that you're paying back, and from the difference between your interest rate and the interest rate the bank is being charged for the money they borrow from a money wholesaler to give to you. The wholesaler lends money to the bank at a lower rate than the one the bank charges you, the end borrower, and the bank pockets the difference. This is known as the "interest rate spread".

When it comes to real estate loans, the two most important institutions responsible for wholesale money borrowing by banks are the Federal National Mortgage Association (informally known as Fanny Mae) and Federal Home Loan Mortgage Corporation (aka Freddy Mac).

After a bank gives you and a bunch of other people real estate loans, it sells your debt to Fannie May or Freddie Mac. You may not know it, but you actually owe money not to the bank that issued the loan to you, but to the agency that bought it from the bank! Even that is not the complete picture because having bought the loans from your bank, Fannie May and Freddie Mac bundle them up further into even larger packages and translate them into bond offerings, traded on such national markets as the New York Stock Exchange. These bonds, in turn, are bought and re-sold by pension funds, insurance companies, and all kinds of other players, including foreign governments and major private investors.

In order to be purchased by the wholesaler agency, a mortgage must meet certain cut-off criteria. These criteria determine whether or not the loan qualifies as "conventional" or "Jumbo".

Today the conventional loan limit is $453,100. Jumbo loans are $679,650, or 150% of the conventional loan. Jumbo mortgages are handled by the insurance companies, pension funds, and other such organizations directly. Mortgages above that limit are referred to as "super Jumbo" - but these are rare.

Across the United States, conventional loans statistically predominate, representing 96% of all mortgages. But not in New York City. Being a high-cost area, New York City relies mostly on Jumbo loans.

Mortgages are available with fixed or adjustable rates and offer loan terms usually from 5 to 30 years. Just so you understand the lingo, Fixed-Rate Mortgages are often referred to by an acronym: FRM, and their adjustable-rate cousins are known as ARM. The adjustable-rate mortgage is often preferable for a number of reasons. First, it comes with a much lower interest rate for its first term, compared to a fixed-rate mortgage. With an adjustable-rate mortgage, you can select the length of that initial term lasting anywhere from one to ten years—and during that period your interest rate actually does not change. A very interesting thing happens when the initial term has run its course. The mortgage converts to the new, higher rate - however, the actual amount you are paying under these new conditions is calculated based on the remaining payment, not on the entire amount you've originally borrowed. So, if you've been paying off your mortgage well, you will probably end up paying less per month than before, even after your mortgage rate goes up!

Usually there's no requirement for the monthly mortgage insurance if your down-payment is 20% of the property price or higher (and I do recommend that your down payment should be at least 20%). However, if your down payment is below 20%, the mortgage insurance becomes obligatory but cancelable when your equity reaches 20%.

This is pertinent only to prime residence mortgage loans, which banks can finance up to 80% of the cost. If it's a "second home" or "investment property", the banks expect the down-payment to be at least 50 %.

So, what are the actual mechanics of the process of applying for a mortgage?

After you've assessed your financial situation, do your research and find a highly reputable, experienced mortgage broker.

Theoretically, this step can be skipped and you could go straight to a bank - but I don't recommend it. A good mortgage broker has so much to offer, and you will probably save a noticeable amount of money by not bypassing this step.

The mortgage broker (or a bank clerk) will interview you about your financial situation and will help you obtain a mortgage pre-approval letter. It's a simple preliminary document that states that you're preapproved to a bank loan up to a certain amount at a certain interest rate. The pre-approval letter carries very little weight. Mostly, it gives the seller's team and yours the sense that you're taking the whole thing seriously enough - and also gives you the initial idea of your probability to qualify for the necessary loan.

Your next step is obtaining the mortgage commitment letter. As I wrote above, ideally you should obtain this document before you even find a piece of property that you know you want to buy. In that case, you will have some extra leverage with the seller. This is in spite of the fact that the bank is likely to include certain "subject to" clauses in this document. For example "subject to underwriter's review" - which means that later, upon reviewing your credit more closely, the bank may still say no. Often you may request a commitment letter after your offer to buy a piece of property has already been accepted. To obtain the mortgage commitment letter, you provide the bank with a lot of financial information. If you're requesting the commitment letter with a specific piece of property in mind, you'll also be asked to pay for getting the property inspected and appraised, and once the bank is confident it meets the proper standards, you will receive the mortgage commitment letter.

The next small step is important, and it's a good example of why you should have a very experienced support team when you're working out any real estate deal. I recommend that any real estate investor (or rather, an attorney acting on behalf of the investor, also supported by the real estate broker,) extend every effort to include a so-called "mortgage contingency" clause into your contract. Although this clause isn't easy to negotiate, it guarantees that you're secured from the situation in which, for any reason other than your own fault, you're unable to obtain financing for your purchase, but the seller pockets your deposit anyway.

Now let's take a closer look at quite another dimension of mortgages: those for commercial real estate.

One important counterintuitive concept you must understand is the penalty involved in paying back your **commercial** mortgage too early. Banks actually don't want you to take a mortgage loan and pay it off right away. This makes the whole business of approving you for a loan unprofitable for them. (There's an entire industry based on re-selling mortgages as bonds to other countries. What would they re-sell if everyone suddenly paid off the entire loan amounts?) So, banks came up with a system of penalties for loan holders too eager to increase their equity.

If you've taking a mortgage on a residential property and realize that you can pay all of it or some of it sooner than expected, then you're in luck: there are no pre-payment penalties on residential mortgages. That's why I do recommend, if possible, to pay back your mortgage as quickly as possible - if you can, much sooner than the duration of the mortgage. This will greatly expand your subsequent options. You'll be able to refinance or get a blanket mortgage for the next purchase by simply providing the current property as collateral. There's no downside to paying your residential mortgage early!

You will, however, incur penalties if you absolutely must pre-pay a *commercial* mortgage. First of all, you absolutely cannot pre-pay a commercial mortgage within the first 6 months. After six months, the penalty is the highest: up to 3 points. After the first year, it becomes 2 points and then finally 1 point.

Between 2002 and 2007 we saw that all a buyer needed to do in order to be able to get a mortgage loan was just ask. Deals were closed instantly - and only much later did the reason for this become clear: the market for secondary mortgages that had been packaged and resold went into countries that didn't even know anything about mortgages but just bought them instead as bonds.

That practice existed for over 5 years and caused the reality we were forced to face over the subsequent years: the crisis of the entire banking system.

As a consequence of those "easy mortgages", many hopeful homeowners in America lost their homes. This was a punch in the gut of the American dream of owning real estate, since the majority of homeowners were left absolutely without equity on their houses or apartments. They were sometimes forced to abandon their houses, or couldn't re-finance their mortgages. While waiting for the appraisal to refinance, they often lost their property, which was taken away by the banks after the homeowners received foreclosure notices. In some areas of the United States real estate prices have still not risen again to the artificial heights reached by these mortgages during the "real estate bubble."

To exacerbate the situation, the system of recording mortgages in many jurisdictions nationwide—including New York City during the first decade of the new millennium—was badly outdated and deeply flawed, due to a giant loophole. The offices of the city registers didn't require any verification to the information submitted to it. That allowed a number of unethical individuals over a certain prolonged period of time (for years!) to give themselves fake deeds to any properties they had their eyes on, and obtain sizeable mortgages from the banks! Nationwide, lender losses from mortgage fraud totaled over $800 million per year! -and New York was one of the top 10 mortgage fraud states.

The situation culminated in the famous public experiment, or rather, publicity stunt, conducted by the Pulitzer Prize-winning investigative reporter and Emmy Award-winning television correspondent William Sherman in December 2008, when he managed to "steal" a piece of real estate property from its rightful owner and obtain full ownership with New York City's consent. Which property? None other than the Empire State Building. William Sherman claimed that it took him all of 90 minutes to transfer the deed from Empire State Land Associates to the bogus Nelots Properties, LLC ("Nelots" is "stolen", spelled backwards) - and the city approved it!

The mortgage industry today is changing, as it has continued to change since 2009, when many banks that gave out easy mortgages either went out of business or had been absorbed by bigger banks. Fleet Bank and Merrill Lynch merged with Bank of America, and Washington Mutual merged with J.P. Morgan Chase. Many banks were fined and settlements were offered to the homeowners who suffered in the crisis.

Banks have learned their lesson. Today they give mortgages without any risk to themselves; you can only get mortgage if you have good income and solid credit. Both will be thoroughly checked before a decision is made. It's crucial for the bank to confirm that the buyer is qualified and will pay back the mortgage and that the payments will remain steady throughout the entire duration of the mortgage - all 30 years, if we're talking about residential mortgages.

Banks use credit scores to determine if borrowers are a "good risk." Many mortgage products today have minimum credit score criteria that would qualify the borrowers for the mortgage loan - or not. Your credit score is examined and reported by credit bureaus: TransUnion, Equifax and Experian.

There are still banks that give mortgages with very low interest rates (2.5% or lower). Another great thing about the mortgage situation today is that you don't pay mortgage broker fees like before. It's good for the consumer that a residential mortgage broker is typically paid by the bank, and not by you.

I recommend that you find out in detail what expenses you're going to incur when taking your mortgage. Some expenses are obligatory, while others are less than typical. For example, a bank will ask you to pay for an appraisal, but it shouldn't request an application fee. You should be able to start the process of your mortgage application without paying the bank anything for that.

It's a good idea to obtain your HUD (banking statement that describes all your mortgage expenses - also known as "settlement statement"). That's a standard form used in America, displaying all itemized services and fees charged to the borrower by the lender or broker.

Shop around! There's always some new bank that is offering a brand-new special program that could be suitable for your needs. Mortgage brokers usually know everything about such programs and banks. That's why I recommend that you consider enlisting the help of a mortgage broker, rather than talking to a bank. As a rule, a mortgage broker will help you save money. Your mortgage broker is one of the key members of your investing team.

Do compare the rate offered by mortgage brokers with those that are offered directly by banks. You may stumble into a bank that offers such excellent terms that a mortgage broker may become redundant. That's seldom the case though.

Typically, one of your team members (a real estate broker or an attorney) will refer to you a good mortgage broker. I recommend that you take time to interview that mortgage broker in detail. How fast can the mortgage broker formalize the financing; what deals has that broker made recently with the lender that they recommend approaching; are there any hidden fees; will the mortgage broker be present at the closing?

Remember, you can request HUD from the bank or from your mortgage broker.

From the moment you apply for mortgage to the closing of the deal, your mortgage broker will stay with you. Typically, mortgage brokers do visit the closings, and you really want them to be there because you want to make sure there are no surprise fees during this final, most important ritual in real estate. I had personally walked away from a few closings because suddenly I saw a surprise bank payment that had not been mentioned to me before. It's important that there are no surprises like that.

Developers face an entirely different task compared to investors.

Developers who use the property get some upside because through renovation and construction the property grows in value. Developers receive project financing from banks, and they're interested not in LTV (loan-to-value) amount, but in LTC (loan-to-cost). Banks give developers money not only to purchase property, but also for construction work - and that gives developers the opportunity to refinance after they have completed the construction. That type of financing (project financing) is usually relatively short-term (24-36 months), and there are a lot of lenders that specialize in the project financing niche.

When it comes to real estate loans, there are two kinds of money in real estate, "easy" and "hard". Easy money is any loan with interest rate below 6%. Hard money is loans with 6% interest rate and above.

There's a whole hard money industry always next to real estate. You hear real estate people say "hard money lenders" often. A typical hard money loan includes 10% interest rate and 3% origination fee - the money that the lender instantly takes. This may seem as if hard money lenders are just loan sharks, but without this industry real estate wouldn't even exist, and often we see projects that are financed like this. These are usually the hottest projects. Please bear in mind that as an investor, you sometimes won't be able to access finances from anyone other than hard money lenders.

Every once in a while, I encounter a situation where an investor is pressed to close the title within a very short time. Usually that happens when the property has been bought off auction or from a foreclosure, and the seller "holds a gun to the investor's head". The investor must close fast, and the bank would be happy to provide the mortgage, but knowing the pressing deadline, the bank will attempt to take advantage of you and offer the interest rate of 8% or even above 10%. (We usually see this in commercial properties.) In situations like this, any garden-variety, friendly neighborhood bank may suddenly turn into a hard-money lender. Having closed the deal, investors almost immediately begin to seek refinancing at a lower percentage.

We'll talk about auctions now, and refinancing a bit later in this chapter. Auctions are a new angle, but ultimately, it's just a different manifestation of the same set of key principles.

Auctions

I know many real estate investors who don't like auctions, wouldn't go anywhere near an auction even if you paid them, and would never buy auctioned property because the common belief is that one can never obtain a piece of property via an auction at a right price.

I understand where they're coming from, but I disagree. I often visit auctions, enjoy them, and know how to benefit from them. Yes, there's the excitement of the moment that's not unlike gambling, and some people may be prone to making mistakes. But that's on the surface. Underneath all that superficial stuff, I find that auctions can serve as a perfect example of what it's like to engage in strategic thinking in real estate. In fact, I treat auctions as a sort of "real estate dojos" where I fine-tune my strategic and tactical skills.

It's my belief that any auction reflects the entire dynamic of the real estate market. Good properties can and should be bought during auctions, and inevitably whenever I visit an auction, I always find a good well-priced deal for myself and my investors.

(I should add that in my opinion, auction prices are very good indicators of the actual value of any property.)

There are no special methods or techniques for auctions that differ much from regular real estate investment game. The only difference is speed, and the need for strict control over one's mind and emotions.

An investor should always come to an auction well-prepared and having done extensive homework. You should know the maximum price you're prepared to pay and for what kind of property - both the price and property type should fit your long-term goals. It's crucial that, notwithstanding any influence, pressure, emotional manipulation, or any other external factors or nuances, you do not go above the target price that you were prepared to pay.

You also always go to auctions knowing your exit strategy: what you're going to do with the property you're going to buy, how long you're going to keep it, when and for how much money you're going to sell it - or maybe you wouldn't wish to sell it at all, and it will just become a beautiful new addition to your portfolio of properties.

There are many types of auctions: bankruptcy auctions, municipal auctions, sheriff sales, US treasury sales, and many others. If you are interested in such sales, I'd recommend that you sign up for property auction email alerts. This will keep you aware of all the events. Even if you can't take part in each and every one of them, knowing what properties are up for auction offers an excellent mirror of the local real estate market. Thanks to auction alerts, you will know what kinds of properties are available, and what you can buy and sell - and you will sharpen your intuitive understanding of the real estate market.

The most important thing is probably being aware of the inventory of foreclosed properties that you can buy at foreclosure auctions. Going to such an auction, you must know the lien amount (also known as "upset amount") - the minimum bid with which the auction opens. The seller will not be ready to accept a lesser amount.

It's important to participate in the final foreclosure sales, so that you don't encounter any problems with your title. It's up to you to make sure that, as per the terms of the auction; you will receive the final foreclosure and don't have to do any additional work relative to obtaining the rights of ownership.

Title closing after foreclosure auctions typically happen within 30 days. That's not a lot of time, and you and your entire team must be ready to act fast in order to close that deal.

It would be appropriate to mention at this point that there are auctions (usually these are sheriff or US treasury auctions) where you're buying the right to close within 3 days! At such auctions, it's assumed that you buy a bargain and come to the auction practically with the entire amount of money in your pocket. You will only have 3 days to examine the deal and the validity of every document. In many cases, all the information about such an auction and its terms are fully available before-hand, but there are situations when no such information is provided and you go to the auction knowing that you will be taking a risk. In that case, you'd be risking your 10% deposit.

Sometimes you may find out about an auction on the day that it's being held. If you're really interested in a property that suddenly became available on great terms, don't be surprised to find yourself rushing to a bank to get a bank-certified check for 10% of the maximum final bid. Once that's done, you just catch your breath, regroup, refocus your mind, and prepare to participate. Having the bank-certified check with 10% of your maximum bid in your pocket, and knowing that this is your only and final offer - gives structure to your bidding and can develop great discipline in you as a real estate investor.

Sellers or lawyers representing banks in control of the properties being auctioned always come to the auction with serious intentions. Both sides - the seller and the buyer - know that the deal will be reached, and the price to satisfy both parties will be found on the day of the auction. Whatever their passions maybe, and however many bids may be received, the sale will take place, and the deal will be concluded on the spot.

Auction locations can be very official, and sometimes they're dramatic and picturesque. They can be held in a courthouse lobby or even on the steps outside under an open sky, with all the bidders standing on their feet rather than sitting comfortably in chairs. An auctioneer may also ask you to present the check, to demonstrate to the auction the seriousness of your intentions.

In the unlikely event that you bid above the amount you originally planned to spend (my advice is to not do that, but there are exceptions) - you should be prepared to do a quick dash to the nearest branch of your bank so you can bring the money within 45 minutes of winning the bid. Also be on the lookout for auctions that do not have a reserved price - often these are bargain auctions, and you can make an extremely successful purchase at one of them.

Speaking of the money above what you were prepared to spend - how much does it cost to buy real estate in New York City? (I'm not talking about real estate prices or cost per square footage, but about something much more mundane: the actual cost associated with closing a real estate deal).

Closing Costs

You better brace yourself, here's what you will have to pay for:

1. Appraisal fee
2. Bank legal fees
3. Bank underwriting fee
4. Buyer's lawyer cost
5. Common charges to the end of the current month
6. Condominium board application
7. Condominium credit report
8. Credit report fee
9. Mansion Tax (from 1% on properties costing between $1 and $2 million to 3.9% on properties over $25 million in price)

10. Mortgage points (1-2% of loan - or more, if you'd like to lower your interest rate)
11. Mortgage tax
12. Mortgage to the end of the current month
13. Move-in deposit
14. Move-in fee
15. Real estate tax, prepaid up to six months
16. Mortgage recording charge (1.8% of the mortgage amount for loans under $500k or 1.925% for loans above that)
17. Title insurance (about .5% of the purchase price)
18. Title search
19. Transfer taxes, if you're buying a new condo (0.4% of purchase price for properties costing from under $1,000,000 to $2,999,999, and 0.65% for anything more expensive)

All of this will cost you a pretty penny. It's worth it though, and don't be jealous of the seller, as they're obligated to pay their fair share, too.

Quite a few condo buildings nowadays may require that, in addition to the above, you also place a year or two worth of common charges in the escrow account for extra security against possible non-payment. The likelihood of this happening depends largely on your debt-to-income ratio, the percentage of your down payment, your status in the US, and other similar factors.

I'd like you to gain a very practical takeaway from this: even if you're well off, the kind of money you must be prepared to pay for a real estate transaction isn't negligible. You probably wouldn't want to spend that much too often. This means that you should only spend it strategically, with the view several years ahead down the line. Think of the apartment you're about to buy as a time machine of sorts. You're buying it for the older you.

Are you planning to get married, or are you looking for an apartment because you recently got married and now plan to have kids? Buy an apartment with that goal in mind, with room to grow in the neighborhood that would suit your needs a few years into the future, otherwise you'll have to spend the same or a higher amount of money in closing costs again just because you didn't plan far enough into the future.

Now let's talk about something we all love.

Real Estate Taxes

I recently read an interesting article authored by one of the most successful real estate investors operating in Florida, who expressed the paradoxical idea that we should want to pay more taxes.

Why?

Well, the author explained, you certainly don't want to pay more taxes than strictly necessary, but when you do pay the absolute legal minimum taxes, you want to strive to pay more taxes every next year because that means your gross profit keeps increasing. This also means your business contributes not only to your success, but also to the well-being of everyone around you.

I must say, he has a point.

Property taxes that you pay as a Manhattan real estate investor are crucial for New York City's prosperity. They also represent one of the biggest expenses associated with owning real estate property. Unfortunately, not a lot of people can boast of having any real clarity in their understanding of real estate taxes. Fortunately, you won't be among those people any longer, because right now I'm going to explain to you all the most important things you should know about property taxes.

We pay property taxes to cover the cost of community services, such as school construction, park maintenance, and police salaries. They also support municipal workers and the local and state governments: the city hall, the school board, county governments, and so on. In 2017, New York City collected $28.7 billion in property taxes, enough to pay the salaries of all 325,000 of all city employees. 53% of all the taxes collected to the city are attributable to real estate.

The amount of property tax you'll have to pay is based on the assessed value of your property.

How do you find out what taxes you're going to pay? This is where I, as a real estate broker, can shine and deliver maximum value to you. In fact, one of the most important reasons for enlisting a broker is that they can help you correctly determine the assessed value of the property, the local tax rate, the amount the current owner is paying in taxes, and whether the current owner has exceptions that may be transferred to you…or not.

Another important thing to consider is whether you'd be paying a fair amount of taxes compared to your neighbors. A skilled, experienced broker can help with that as well. If the property you're about to buy is beset with taxes that are significantly higher than similar properties within the same city block, you can challenge the assessment by filing the appropriate application in the assessor's office.

Here's a very important thing to know about real-estate related taxes: you're allowed to (and therefore, you should!) deduct from your income taxes the amount of interest you're paying on your mortgage with the maximum principal up to $1 million.

There are multiple types of tax exemptions, often unique to the property or the neighborhood. We discussed some of these earlier in the book. Usually they are offered to a property developer by the city in exchange for meaningful work that benefits the city and public in some ways. There are also special tax breaks to military veterans, seniors, and other groups.

There's a lot more to taxes, and I could write an entire book covering just the tax aspect of real estate. But my main message to you as an investor is that when you consider purchasing a piece of real estate, you must know what taxes you're going to pay for it. You don't want that figure to come as a surprise.

I'd like to dedicate the next section of this chapter to the special set of circumstances faced by foreigners who would like to sell or buy real estate in the United States.

Foreign Investors

I hope you agree with my philosophy that any real estate purchase should be highly strategic. As you invest in your property, you must be focused on a clearly defined goal and think several moves ahead. This goes double if you happen to hail from outside the U.S. Being a foreigner, you will face more challenges in obtaining a mortgage from a U.S. bank, as well as a somewhat more complex real estate tax structure than the one applicable to a regular American real estate investor.

If you're not a US citizen or permanent resident, to find it easier to get your mortgage application approved by an American bank, I recommend trying to establish a relationship with one or several such banks without even leaving your home country. If the bank knows you well as their customer, they will have fewer reasons to say no to your request of a loan.

When you buy property, typically you don't pay transfer taxes. I emphasize "typically" because every deal is unique and it's quite possible that a property may include great advantages for you, but in return the seller will demand that you cover the transfer taxes. This doesn't happen often, but it *can* happen.

Usually though, it's the seller's responsibility to pay the transfer taxes. Which is good news for you when you buy the property.

Or is it?

Look ahead a few years, when you're likely to become the seller. The amount of taxes you pay when you sell your property depends on how you bought it, and quite a number of other factors. There are many traps that you should be careful to avoid.

Let's start with the title. You can obtain the title of your property in your own name - or register it to a business entity. There are advantages to taking a title in your own name. When you sell your property later, (provided that you held on to it for longer than one year), your gain from the property will be taxed as a long-term capital gain, at the rate of 15%. However, if the owner of the property who holds the title under your own name passes away, anything in excess of $60,000 will be taxed at the rate of up to 45%.

Americans and permanent residents of the United States have it easy by comparison because any property up to $2 million in price currently exists under a standard tax exemption. So, when an American citizen passes away the property under $2 million will not be subject to taxes at all. Additionally, citizens and permanent residents can pass all their property to their spouses, tax-free.

Registering a corporation is a decent alternative - there are ways to save on taxes and even get tax returns. You can form an LLC, a C-Corporation, or a Limited Partnership. A foreigner cannot register an S-Corporation in the United States. That said, you absolutely must discuss the issue of forming a corporation with your broker, attorney, accountant, and other members of your investor's team - especially with your title expert.

Some of the countries have peculiar Tax Treaties with the United States, and this may result in double or even triple taxation for a corporate owner of the property. Canada, for example, is one of such countries. If you're from Canada, you'll probably be better off owning your property as yourself.

When you invest in a property other than just your prime residence, chances are you'll probably have tenants in that property. I most certainly hope you do!

I also hope that you file all your taxes - on time. Because, as a foreigner owning rental property, you're entitled to the so-called "net election", which allows you to only pay tax on the net rental income, and deduct all property related expenses and losses (maintenance, depreciation, etc.). You only qualify for all these things on the condition that you file your taxes on time! For example, a foreigner unfamiliar with the severity of the United States tax laws and owning a rental property that happens to be unprofitable may decide to not file tax documents because they've been losing money. That person will lose the privilege of the "net election" - and will receive a letter from the IRS informing them that they're now obligated to pay a federal income tax of 30% of the gross rent with no deduction for any business expense. When you sell your property, you'll be shocked to discover that you won't be able to use any of your business losses, throughout the entire duration of property ownership, to reduce the capital gain tax on sale.

Obviously, if you're serious about your real estate investment in the United States, and your investor's team is solid, things like that are not likely to happen to you. If you plan your taxes and maintain meticulous compliance with the United States tax law, you will not only achieve high tax efficiency, but will gain greater return on your real estate investment. Your team is what will make all the difference - that's why we've dedicated the entire next chapter to it.

Sooner or later, the day may come when you decide to sell your property. In preparation for that day, you should become familiar with a very important law that governs sales by foreigners of real estate properties in the United States. It's called FIRPTA, an acronym that stands for Foreign Investment in Real Property Tax Act.

It's a very interesting and fairly simple law. Under FIRPTA, when you, a foreign investor, sell your property in the United States, the IRS must receive 10% of the gross sale price, and essentially hold on to that money. Sending that money to the IRS is the responsibility of the closing agent, the attorney, or the title company handling the sale. The IRS will withhold the money until the tax document is filed, and later will send it back to you - minus the taxes you owe.

This law ensures that the choice of paying or not paying taxes on the sale of property is pretty much taken away from the foreigner who sells it - by making the supporting parties acting in the deal legally obligated to withhold your money and send it to the escrow account that belongs to the IRS. In fact, by law, the closing agent and/or the title company finalizing the deal are required to explicitly ask the seller whether or not they're foreign!

This is where we must ask: what's a "foreigner"?

FIRPTA applies the slightly sci-fi sounding term "nonresident alien individual" to any person who is neither a United States citizen nor a resident of the United States. What exactly does that actually mean?

According to FIRPTA, you may be from any country in the world, but would be considered a United States resident if you've been physically present in the United States for 183 days or longer during the calendar year. The "183 days or longer" is known as "substantial presence". If you meet that requirement, the closing agent won't have to take away the 10% and send it to the IRS. Instead, it will be assumed that you are a law-abiding person and would willingly pay normal American taxes.

Ditto if you have the "green card" - more formally known as the United States Permanent Resident Card (USCIS Form I-551). If you have one then the 10% withholding doesn't apply.

In all the other cases, you're subject to FIRPTA withholding, and your closing agent has 20 days after the title close to report the deal to the IRS using the famous Form 8288.

However, there are a few interesting exceptions that may change things for you. For example, if you are certain that the 10% FIRPTA withholding is much higher than your true tax liability, you can file a special application with the IRS and request a reduced withholding. Please note that this happens after the 10% has already been withheld. If the IRS determines that all the information is correct and properly presented in your application, they will return the difference between the full 10% and the amount of tax that you actually owe within a fairly short period of time.

If you don't file such an application, they will return that difference later anyway. On the other hand, if the amount of tax you own is higher than 10%, you may discover that you have to pay additional tax. Well, *c'est la vie!*

Another common exception applies to a piece of property that a foreigner sells for less than $300,000 to a buyer who plans to use it as their prime residence and reside at that property for at least 50% of time it's being used for at least the two following years. In that case, no 10% withholding is required. But that exception probably wouldn't apply to you if you're selling property in Manhattan - I don't think you can find anything for under $300,000. (But please let me know if you do. I'd like to see that property.)

Whether you're a foreigner, a permanent resident, or a citizen of the United States, thank you for having read this section. The point I wanted to make by writing it was that there are a lot of tax-related issues to consider when you purchase your property. You must foresee all of these matters when you make your purchase. Only then can you truly succeed as a real estate investor.

So either via regular sale or through an auction, you've acquired a great piece of property. You've bought in strategically - keeping your financial goals in mind, planning for taxes and additional expenses. You bought your property well.

Now what?

Passive Income

Generating passive income is one of the most important advantages of any investment, including investing in real estate. When you invest money in the stock market, bonds, or an IRA account, you don't have to work in order to be paid a salary. You are free to do as you please, and the money comes to you.

What makes it possible?

When I was young in Russia, I saw other children around me being conditioned to believe that money is made by selling your time and effort. Later on I found out that you could sell everyday goods for money. I had my "aha!" moment when I discovered real estate and realized money could be made by *owning* a large object that has valuable physical properties and selling these *physical properties* over time, while still owning the object.

Intrigued?

There's a fundamental principle you must grasp about money. Money is the equivalent of one of the three things: change, mass, or information.

You can sell your time, during which you expend your energy to bring about a certain result (which means, you create change). Or you can own a physical object that has a useful mass, which you can sell over the course of a certain period of time. Or you can have knowledge (information).

Of these three methods for obtaining money, owning physical mass is the one that generates passive income. Simply by the virtue of owning it, you generate income, but time has to pass for that income to grow. That's why you get your checks every month.

Now let's get practical. I may be biased, but in my opinion real estate is the best form of investment for generating passive income. Your tenants work to ensure your cash flow: regular, consistent, steady, guaranteed. All four words are a variation of the same thing: every month you receive envelopes containing your new money. And New York City is the ideal market for this passive income because it's a high-occupancy rental market - one of the highest in the world!

For example, the average rental occupancy rate in Battery Park City is 90%. The neighborhood features very strong local economies and a low unemployment rate, and Manhattan in general is a high per-capita income community.

The best ways to generate passive income via real estate is to buy rent-ready property, or to make renovations and prepare the property for rent personally. When you prepare the property for renting it out, all of your expenses are tax-deductible. Also, when you prepare property for occupancy, you can obtain low-interest loans. Banks will gladly give you home improvement loans, which usually feature much lower interest rates than regular loans or credit cards. You can use a home improvement loan to prepare your property for rent, and then your tenants pay back the loan. Your tenants, by virtue of paying regular rent, automatically help you to build equity in the property.

You can manage your property personally or you can delegate it to a property manager who will do that for you.

You can usually lease your property for one or two years. If you provide the one-year lease agreement with the option to renew, I recommend that you clearly indicate what the market rate will be for the second year. If you neglect to do this, you may set yourself up for a potential legal battle with your tenant over the next year's rent - and you definitely do not want a judge to tell you what market rate should be set for your property. This will be one of those things that truly "echoes in eternity", and might come back to bite you in more ways than you can imagine for years to come. Spending thirty seconds to indicate the market rate for the second year in the lease with option to renew prevents all that unpleasantness from ever taking place.

What properties are best for generating passive income? There are many schools of thought regarding that matter. Some investors believe that the best market is residential - after all, people have to live somewhere! Others feel that the American economy is in good shape, and therefore you can always lease a store or a restaurant space.

It is my opinion that the real-life market has demonstrated to us that the Manhattan economy and America change overtime. Today the residential market could be the best, and the office rental market could be under duress, and tomorrow, shockingly, retail market leases may outpace residential. Up until 2015, for example the retail sector grew and prices for it grew. There was a huge retail boom, which then reversed into the current slump it is experiencing. Today some experts bet on office spaces, and others postulate that hotels and extended-stay hotels are the most interesting and promising sector.

I recommend that my clients invest in mixed-use properties. That's what banks do today, often investing in a property that's comprised of multiple sectors: residential/multifamily, retail, hotel, office, and so on. For example, the Four Seasons in Tribeca has a retail component, a parking garage, condominiums, and a hotel.

We covered the intelligent approach to buying property, multiple challenges related to mortgages, taxes, being a foreigner, and ways to generate passive income. Our next section is equally important.

To Sell, or Not to Sell - That is The Question

Well, that's not really that much of a question. The answer is, do not sell. Keep your property and use it for passive income. That's it. Alas, there are actually multiple factors every real estate investor must take into consideration in order to answer that question correctly on a case-by-case basis.

Some years ago, I used to enjoy chatting with a gentleman who operated mostly out of an old bar and owned a few properties here and there in the West Village. *Quite* a few properties, actually, maybe slightly over a hundred buildings, which he bought around 1985 for about a million dollars. By the turn of the millennium their value grew to a couple of hundred million, and today they're worth a tad over a billion dollars. Back then, he seemed really old and wise to me, and I hoped to learn a lot about real estate from his mentorship. Unfortunately, I missed that great opportunity because shortly after I met that man, he passed away. He was 64 at the time of his demise, and today I think that he was too young. His name was Bill Gottlieb.

Bill used to say that he learned real estate at the feet of Harry Helmsley, who had been a figure of mythical proportions and a former owner of the Empire State Building, among a few other interesting properties. According to Bill Gottlieb, Harry Helmsley had a mantra: "Never sell!"

Bill followed his mentor's advice fanatically and indeed never sold a single property he ever owned.

There are many old families in New York City that hold on to their buildings and do not sell, preferring steady cash flow from their tenants. Good fortune has brought me in contact with some of these families, and every once in a while I help them with various matters related to their properties. Often these families, in addition to keeping their current buildings, invest in new construction. This, for example, was the *modus operandi* of the late Leonard Litwin of Glenwood Management, who developed and managed only rental buildings.

There's also The Durst Organization. They never sell but always refinance their buildings, and using that strategy they have amassed a huge fortune - and an even more spectacular portfolio. For example, when the city needed a billion dollars to invest in Downtown, it came to The Durst Organization, which happened to have the necessary excess cash from the recent refinancing of their iconic Bank of America Tower at One Bryant Park. As a result, the city got their cash and The Durst Organization became the proud owner of the Freedom Tower at One World Trade Center. As far as real estate deals go, this one is comparable in its simplicity and classic beauty to Beethoven's Ninth Symphony.

My take on this: as a rule, if you can afford not to sell today, it's best not to, even if the market is at its lowest and prices are at their highest. Inevitably, the value of your properties will only increase, and at the next similar cycle of the market your property will cost a lot more. So, wait at least until the next period of high prices, or the next one after that. Just be aware that cycles may last a long time and you may have to wait many years.

You may ask: if we know that the long-term value of your property is only going to increase - could there even be a good reason to sell it?

Yes. If you're in a financial situation so dire that your property has become a massive liability rather than an asset, you should probably sell it. If you're selling your property because things are not going well, do me a favor and give me a buzz. Maybe I can help. There are situations that may appear like perfect hell, but I have experience in turning things around for my clients, and sometimes there are easy solutions to what may seem like insurmountable problems. Who knows, perhaps together we can turn that sale of property you're considering into a new cycle of prosperity in your family's life.

You don't have to be in trouble to sell your property. I can actually think of many positive reasons to sell. If the sale of an old property will bring you prosperity, selling it may be to your advantage. For example, you may discover a perfect opportunity to acquire an excellent new property, but you can only afford buying if you sell what you currently own. In this perfect match scenario, you'll be selling to buy. If you find yourself in a situation where you know that you can hit such a "growth spurt" in your real estate ownership - my advice is: take the risk.

In fact, here's some general advice that comes from many years of experience. Always take risks. Risk pays off. Use the liquidity of the Manhattan real estate market -it's comparable to that of the stock market, but in real estate your risk is lower and it's easier to foresee and plan for your success. Real estate is a game of skill, where you should have the clarity of mind, patience, and reflexes comparable to those of a warrior.

Refinancing

We already discussed an important principle that you should always adhere to when you invest in real estate: the "earn as you buy". Let's now press on and assume that you've already found the appealing property, put down the upfront payment and taken out a mortgage for the rest of the cost. You're now a property owner.

This may appear somewhat counterintuitive, but in real estate you don't have to buy new properties or sell the ones that you already own in order to make money. Sometimes all you have to do is collect money from the property you already own and then... keep the property. You can do it as many times as you want, while continuously increasing the value of your investment - and the best part is, every time you get new cash, that money will be tax-free.

Intrigued? *Refinancing* is the technique that allows you to achieve all these things. How does it work?

Over time, the market value your property will undoubtedly grow. This will happen due to a shift from a buyers' market to a sellers' market, thanks to the improvements or renovations you've made. Perhaps you've added square footage, or a new design. Simply put, in the long term, real estate prices in Manhattan will rise.

Whatever the reason for the growth may be, you can have your property re-appraised and receive tax-free cash to the entire amount above the original price of your property. That's called refinancing. Another way to look at refinancing: you are trading in your current mortgage for a new one with better terms - and the difference comes in the form of tax-free cash.

Refinancing a mortgage is one of the most important tasks that you can undertake as a real estate investor. It's so important, in fact, that I'd describe it as your duty to yourself and your family. It will positively affect not only your monthly cash flow, but also the market value of your property. Even though the refinancing process can be expensive and time-consuming, it's worth every dollar and minute you invest in it. You must plan ahead and make refinancing a solid part of your strategy. Refinancing allows you to cash out while keeping your property - and that's something you should always strive for as investor.

When you plan to refinance your goals should be the following:

a) Decrease your mortgage percentage rate.
b) Collect as cash the difference between the original real value and the new value of your property.

You'll be glad you did... and be sad if you don't. According to a recent study, every year over 20% of people nationwide who could have benefited from refinancing neglect to use this option and leave a whopping $5.4 billion on the table!

So how do you know if refinancing is right for you? A hint: it most likely is. You should refinance if the following six factors are true:

1. You can get a lower interest rate on the new mortgage.
2. Your equity is 20% or higher.
3. Your debt-to-income ratio is 43% or preferably lower.
4. Your credit score has improved since the time you took out your mortgage.
5. You have the opportunity to get the new mortgage on better conditions that the previous one.
6. You expect to break even before you're ready to sell this property.

As a bonus, here's a quick tip on whether you need to enlist a mortgage broker for your refinancing needs or whether you should "go it alone." If the meaning of all the six points above is perfectly clear to you, you can approach the bank without the assistance of the mortgage broker. Otherwise, enlisting a highly-qualified professional would be to your advantage.

With the assistance of a good mortgage broker you should be able to complete a successful refinancing within 90 days. You can approach one bank or many with a request to evaluate your property and get the most competitive quote. Sometimes it can even be the same bank that gave you the original mortgage loan - if that bank happens to offer a new mortgage program.

What happens then is both simple and pleasant: you close the old mortgage, and take out a brand new one on better terms. Your original lender leaves with a check in hand - and you leave with non-taxable cash in yours, plus a lower interest rate on your new loan. You can use that money however you like. For example, you could acquire more property or add value to the property that you just refinanced. And what's more, you can refinance the same property as many times as you like and as often as you like. I know investors who refinance their property in various perfectly legal ways with different banks as soon as their property grows in value or their equity has increased, or whenever they realize they can get a new mortgage on better terms.

As an alternative, rather than taking away all the money as cash, you can get a so-called equity line of credit: you receive a credit card to be used to the limits of your spending imagination. The advantage of having the equity line of credit is the better annual percentage rate. The best non-equity credit APR is about 10%. You can get 7% if you're very lucky and your credit history and credit score are in particularly good shape. But with an equity line of credit, your APR will be half of that.

Before we move on to the next tool in your investor's arsenal, here's something for you to consider. A bank - any bank - makes money from selling stuff. And what banks sell are "investment opportunities". As a rule, the bank that has given you the mortgage loan will package it and resell it in the form of bonds.

The mortgage is the item that you've received, but what the bank really sells for profit is something called a derivative. Your mortgage may really be owned by a foreign government, or a pension fund, or by a bunch of individuals. And if you happen to have invested in bonds issued by the same bank that gave you the mortgage, you may be a back end investor of your own front end investment. It's like standing between two parallel mirrors and seeing your own reflection endlessly multiplied.

And if you feel that this is a bit surreal, wait until I describe the next simple and useful trick of the trade.

Depreciation

This may sound like a paradox, but while your property grows in value from the point of view of yours and your bank, it also continues to lose value, according to your accountant and the IRS… until all of a sudden it stops losing value, as if by magic - exactly 27 and a half years later (or 39 years, if we're talking about commercial real estate).

This is known as property depreciation - a remarkable feature of American real estate investments, something that doesn't exist in the economies of most of other countries. You can ask your accountant for all of the granular details, but here's nitty-gritty. From Day One of owning a piece of property, over the course of the following 27 and a half years, each year you can write off $1/27.5^{th}$ of that property's value on your taxes, as a token to the "aging" of your investment.

For example, let's say that the value of your property is estimated as $1 million. Divide it by 27.5 —and you get $36,363.63 which is the exact amount you can write off your income tax every year. This is very important for you because if you've invested intelligently, your property should bring you income. And you must pay taxes on that income. Being able to deduct a solid chunk of your property's value from the taxes imposed on it is important.

But you should bear in mind that 27 and a half years later, this will suddenly stop. Why 27 and a half years? In all honesty, I have no idea!

One of the common reasons that real estate owners may want to sell their property is precisely when this 27.5 year period is coming to an end. And since you may not sell the property right away, it's usually listed a few months or a year ahead of time, sometimes more. Experienced property owners aware of market cycles and good at predicting the fluctuations in real estate prices, may want to sell their property well before the end of the depreciation period…And then they usually want to buy a new property immediately thereafter, because then a 27.5 years' years' countdown begins again from zero! In fact, the same goes for the person who bought your former property from you.

Let's take a look at a curious little technique for improving cash flow through managing your taxes in more efficient manner. This is interconnected with the subject we've just discussed.

Cost Segregation

This tax planning strategy once used to be the domain of major commercial real estate management companies and the nation's top accounting firms, but over time it became a universally accepted, highly beneficial practice. Cost segregation involves conducting a special engineering study (known as Cost Segregation Study) that results in a detailed breakdown of costs for your property based on legal and technical details of all the assets. Conducting that study allows you to allocate various costs to multiple recovery periods (such as 5, 7, 15, 27.5 or 39 years). In addition to accelerated tax deductions, you would also benefit from the reduction of estimated quarterly tax payment, property tax savings and transfer tax savings.

Traditionally used for larger commercial properties, cost segregation is a perfectly valid tax planning strategy for residential real estate as well, as long as the price of the property reaches a million dollars or higher (which qualifies practically all properties in Manhattan). Over the last decade, the price for a cost segregation study has gone down by almost 60 percent. Today you can have a cost segregation study performed for you for about $12,000 to $15,000. This seems steep, but it will save you hundreds of thousands of dollars, so it's probably worth considering, don't you think?

To be valid, your cost segregation study must be performed in accordance with the IRS Cost Segregation Audit Techniques Guide and (starting in 2014) with the Tangible Property Regulations.

And now - a very interesting and useful next bit of information.

1031 Exchange

In dealing with both commercial and residential real estate, every investor should be aware of the important concept known as a "like kind" or **1031 Exchange**. Knowing what a 1031 Exchange is and how it works can be a goldmine for you. This past year, the real estate community in the United States had a bit of a scare: people thought that Donald Trump's presidency might result in changes to the 1031 Exchange law. To date he hasn't made any changes to the law—much to the everyone's relief.

Why is this important concept called "1031" and not another number? There's nothing esoteric about it. It's just the number of a chapter in the tax law. The 1031 Exchange was first formulated in 1921, nearly a century ago. The purpose of this law is to create beneficial tax conditions for the owners of real estate properties who want to exchange their property, i.e., sell the old property and immediately buy a new one. This is a barter of sorts, allowing property owners to not pay "capital gain" taxes under certain circumstances.

What circumstances?

It's super-simple. In fact, in the entire messy legal structure of the real estate industry, a 1031 Exchange is the most intuitive law. Just carefully read the next sentence on this page, and you'll grasp its essence. All you need to do is sell your old property and buy a new property *that costs either the same amount of money as your old property - or more.*

That's all there is to it! That's a 1031 Exchange in a nutshell. The law is fairly flexible. For example, rather than buying one new property to replace the old one, you can purchase up to three properties and still not pay any capital gain tax, as long as the combined cost of the new properties is *equal to or higher than* the cost of the property you sold. You can even take advantage of a 1031 Exchange if your new property is cheaper than the old one! - but in that case the balance between the property you sold and the one you've bought is referred to as "taxable boot" and you'll be obligated to pay capital gain tax on it.

Any type of real property you can buy - commercial, residential, hotel, retail, garage, restaurant, triple-net-lease, double-net-lease, multi-family, or even a lot of land with nothing built on it - can by subject to a 1031 Exchange. The only thing you need to remember if you want to bypass the capital gain tax is that your new property must cost the same as or more than the old one. From my point of view, it simply makes no sense to *not* use a 1031 Exchange.

A hypothetical real estate investor who sells a property and *doesn't* use the 1031 Exchange option would lose 18% in Federal taxes and approximately 10% in NY State taxes. So, we're talking about giving away 28% of the profit! And since we assume that the investor in question held onto the property for a number of years, the capital gain could amount to hundreds of thousands or millions of dollars - which the investor would be better off using toward a next real estate purchase.

Now that you understand the core concept, let's dig a little deeper together.

First, some disappointing news. A 1031 Exchange law doesn't apply to your prime residence. But that's not really such bad news, since in the case of a prime residence there's another law in existence that protects you. If you've lived in the property for no less than 2 years, you can write off up to $250,000 in capital gains tax, or up to $500,000 if you're married and file jointly.

(Pretty nifty, no?)

So, as I said, a 1031 Exchange is only applicable to properties that qualify as real estate investments - or to your second home, which is in essence your investment property. Some banks refer to it as an "investment residence" and have special standards for second home mortgages.

The 1031 Exchange law is also fairly lenient. Once you've sold the old property, you have 90 days to identify the new property and 180 days more to close the deal. It doesn't even have to be done within the same fiscal year. The buyer has the opportunity to consider and list up to 3 different possible purchases. This gives you the opportunity to negotiate and reject some of the properties. But this choice doesn't give you extra time, and that's why I always recommend to my investors who are uncertain that they should wait and not get into selling a contract until they find the property to buy. Overall though, four months to identify and close on a new property is usually more than enough.

What makes people want to sell their real estate properties? There could be a number of reasons. Perhaps the property grew in price - or maybe the seller no longer likes this type of property: for example, the seller owned residential property for long time but now wants to invest in commercial real estate.

Or it could have something to do with the depreciation cycle: years have passed since the property was purchased and the owner can now sell it with maximum profit. Since starting on the 28th year the owner stops receiving any tax benefits, he may be motivated to sell.

When you conduct a deal under a 1031 Exchange, you can't just take the money off the table. You must hire an intermediary company - an escrow agent specializing in 1031 Exchange transactions. You should select an experienced specialist, who will usually charge a small sum for his or her services—usually $1,000 - $2,000. They basically hold onto your money from the closing of property you sell to the closing of property (or properties) that you are buying. If you do buy multiple properties, the escrow agent will keep your money until your final closing.

It is the escrow agent who reports the transaction to the IRS, and they also bring the final paycheck to the seller on the day of the closing. The function of the 1031 Exchange escrow agent may be performed by a specialized intermediary company - or by a title company. Sometimes a real estate lawyer does it. A broker cannot serve as an escrow agent though. In any case, I urge you to only deal with highly experienced professionals who have done that type of work before.

The situation can be a bit more complicated if you owned your old property with a partner or multiple partners. You may decide to buy a new property under the 1031 Exchange law, whereas your partner(s) may just want to cash out and not buy the next property.

In that case, the intermediary company will help you to make the sale and calculate the cost of your part of the property. Typically, in such scenarios the old property is sold by a corporation and bought by another corporation, and the job of the intermediary company is to help you correctly document the information on your personal tax return, as well as the corporate tax return. This sounds slightly complicated, but the reality behind it is that you've been only a partial owner of the sold property, and therefore the cost of the new property has to be equal to - or higher than - your share of the cost of the original property.

Can you use financing for a 1031 Exchange deal? Can you, for example, rather than just buying the next property and getting a rollover of the proceeds, instead use the proceeds as a down-payment and get a mortgage on the rest?

Why not? It's beautiful and it's encouraged! Your bank would be glad to use this opportunity to finance your 1031 Exchange deal and give you the necessary leverage. In fact this is one of the ways to achieve explosive growth - and it can make you a much bigger landlord, literally overnight!

Thus the 1031 law gives you the unique opportunity to play "Monopoly", and it reflects the advantages of American capitalism. Buying and selling carefully-selected real estate property, you can own increasingly profitable real estate, earn money as a landlord, finance and refinance the property, increase your equity. All of that gives you ample opportunity to arrive at your desired goal, i.e., your ideal property.

Yes, you can't take it with you, as they say, but you can sure pass it on to your kids and grandkids. And if you bring them up well and choose to include a solid understanding of real estate in their education, then they will benefit from your knowledge and hopefully benefit in myriad ways from your investments.

What if your goal is to buy the Empire State Building?? You may think this is over-reaching, but you can theoretically achieve even such a goal using this method!

In case you're curious, the Empire State Building was in fact transferred for only $1.89 billion in 2013 to Empire State Realty Trust, although offers of $2.2 billion and higher had also been extended. So why not you? Think big!

How often can you do a 1031 exchange? Can you do one every day? Actually, the answer is no.

The condition of a 1031 Exchange is that you must hold onto your property for at least one year before you sell it. Otherwise the IRS characterizes your activity as "real estate speculation," in which case your tax is not considered a "capital gain" but as regular taxable income, which is defined by your tax bracket and could reach as much as 30, 40, or even 50 percent.

As a broker who has worked on numerous 1031 Exchange deals, I always recognize the urgency of closing such transactions and the value of having strong choices among the new properties to purchase. Lately in New York City there has been a noted increase in the number of interstate deals in which clients sold properties out-of-state, for example in Florida, and then bought new properties in Manhattan. All the parties involved in 1031 Exchange deals treat them seriously and when helping a 1031 Exchange buyer I know that the seller or the seller's broker also understands how important it is for us to close the deal on time.

One of my clients was selling his property in Connecticut, where real estate prices really jumped over the last 15 years. The price of his property skyrocketed just around the time he successfully closed his mortgage. And so, he immediately received a lucrative offer to buy that property from his neighbor, even though the property wasn't even on the market.

The client contacted me and requested that I help him find the replacement property which he could buy under the 1031 Exchange law. He was in a bit of a hurry, because his sales contract had already been signed. And because his prime residence was in Manhattan, where else might we look for a new property? When all these factors, including geography came together, we found a good option. As soon as I advertised that I had a 1031 Exchange opportunity on my hands, I was approached by a landlord I'd known for many years. The first thing he asked me was the following: if I sell my property, can you find me a 1031 Exchange as well? It was a bit of a domino effect, and I ended up working simultaneously with the buyer and the seller - and my professional relationship with both continued for many years afterwards.

Parting Ways With a Team Member

I didn't want to diminish the overall positive attitude of the later chapter dedicated to the investor's team - but I find the subject of parting ways with a team member important, so I'm including it here. I do hope, however, that in your real estate investment career you will only encounter top professionals, and will never have to fire anybody.

But you may find yourself in situations where a person you expected top results from just doesn't deliver. This happens in real estate, like in any other industry, and you should be prepared for such situations. The following could be applied to any of your team members, but since I am a real estate broker, I'm going to use a hypothetical case of a real estate investor having to part ways with a broker.

Probably the most important advice I can give you for your relationship with a real estate broker is this: be extremely clear and detailed about mutual expectations, and set it all in writing. If it's not written down and signed, it mustn't be assumed. If something is so important to you that not having it would be a deal-breaker, specify it in writing, and get it signed.

If you must discontinue your relationship with your current real estate broker (or any other member of your real estate investor's team), my recommendation is to discuss that with him or her in person. Emails or text messages are useful as a way to keep the paper trail, but with all their usefulness, they actually limit the probability of coherent dialogue. A conversation in person may untie many seemingly unsolvable knots - often all you need is a little more clarity about mutual expectations! But even if you decide to continue with the original plan to part ways, you'll probably end up doing it on much better terms.

Your contract with a broker will typically include the clause that allows either party to terminate the agreement after 30 days upon giving notice. Most usually, those 30 days can be applied no sooner than 90 days after signing the agreement. Be patient: 30 days, and especially 120 days may seem like a long time if you feel you're losing money due to what you see as your broker's lack of efficiency, but, to misquote King Solomon, that time, too, will pass. And who knows, maybe by that time your broker will deliver the expected results, just when you had given up all hope.

Chapter VII: Sell Cycles and Market Cycles

In my real estate career, there had been several distinct moments when I felt that I had somehow mastered the game, and each time I was careful to remind myself that mastery is an endless process and an illusion. Every real estate transaction is unique and so one of my professional principles is: "beware of generalizations." That being said here are some averages in the Manhattan real estate sales cycle: on average it takes 30 to 60 days to sell a real estate property from the moment it's listed. Typically, there are 5-6 offers to be considered before the property is sold. A broker expects the industry-standard 6% fee, but this becomes increasingly negotiable after a certain property price point.

And that's pretty much it. A sales cycle in real estate is short and straightforward. As for market cycles in Manhattan real estate, they are somewhat more complicated. That's why the entire remainder of this chapter will be dedicated to them.

A real estate property that you plan to buy doesn't exist in a vacuum. It may seem you're paying for the property, but in reality, the price includes a lot more. Whether it's residential or commercial, your new property carries important intangibles: convenience, social status, business growth, family happiness, the future of your children, health, and your lifestyle today and after retirement. If you make the right choices, the quality of your property can positively influence your quality of life.

Which property you buy is crucial, but how you buy it is tremendously important as well. That's why you should study in detail not only the property, but also the circumstances surrounding your deal. The property can be on the market for a considerable period of time - or it may have only been recently listed. The deal could be publicized or private. Or it could be a confidential off-market property that exists under a non-disclosure agreement that no one is supposed to know about.

Does the seller of the property know you - personally or by reputation? Have you bought similar types of property in the past, or maybe in the same neighborhood? Do they feel that they can trust the seriousness of your intentions? Or if you are a first-time buyer—which is a difficult position to be in—do you have solid, iron-clad arguments to persuade the seller that you're just the right buyer for their property? Sometimes the only way for you to acquire the property is to "suck it up" and consciously pay more money for it than it is currently worth. But you also have to plan ahead and know how that property will make you more prosperous and, therefore, how you might sell it in the future.

That's why it's key to understand in what phase of the market - high, middle, or low - you're buying that property.

Now let's dive deeper. The real estate market worldwide goes through cycles, in response to cycles in the world economy. On top of these major waves, there are also local cycles.

New York's real estate market goes through such cycles, and they are especially prominent in Manhattan. Market cycles in Manhattan are *not* regular: a cycle may be longer or shorter, with phases lasting anywhere from 2 to 7 years in duration, with an average of roughly 4 years. This doesn't mean, however, that cycles are random or unpredictable. You can analyze the data and draw useful conclusions.

The Inner Mechanics of the Market Cycle

Market fluctuations in real estate, like in any other industry, depend on changes in supply and demand. When demand exceeds supply, prices go up, and we refer to this as a "sellers' market". When supply exceeds demand, prices go down, and this is known as a "buyers' market". When supply and demand are in perfect balance, it can be a so-called "neutral spot".

The cycle is affected by the available inventory, i.e., what is currently present on the market, as well as the number of offers, new residential and commercial developments, and so on. The main rule for achieving success in real estate investment is very simple: **buy low, sell high.**

The prices are the lowest when supply is abundant; the prices are the highest when inventory is scarce. The market fluctuates between high and low inventory, and therefore between low and high prices. You can make money by using market fluctuations to your advantage.

The language used for describing the situation and the direction of the real estate market can be a little confusing. A couple of paragraphs above, you saw the market described as being controlled by the sellers or buyers. It can also be described as "high vs low" or "soft vs hard".

To understand that terminology, please remember that the "height" of the market refers to supply side. When supply greatly exceeds demand, this is known as a "high market"; this means low prices. When supply is at a maximum, this is known as a "top market" and the prices at that point are the lowest in the cycle. On the other hand, when supply is diminished, this is known as a "low market", i.e., high prices. And when the supply is at its lowest, this is known as a "bottom market". And that's when prices are the highest in a cycle.

The "crest" is the breaking point in the wave. The market is said to "bottom out" when the inventory hits the lowest number and then starts climbing back up again.

A change in market direction can be quite abrupt. The "hardness" or "softness" of the market follows similar logic. A "soft" market is one in which there are more sellers than buyers, and a "hard" market is the opposite.

When everyone wants to sell, it's easiest to negotiate the lowest price. It's best for buyers when there are a lot of offers on the market. But when the market is "devastated" or empty, when there are a lot of buyers with money and when banks give financing fast and easy, sellers celebrate because they can get the highest price for their properties.

Let's dig even deeper!

The supply and demand situation is made somewhat more complex by the existence of a so-called shadow inventory. It's the inventory that's not officially on the market, but which belongs to owners who *wouldn't mind* selling if given the right opportunity. Sometimes these are people who own some special or unique property but don't have a sentimental attachment to it.

Often it's people who initially had the property for sale but couldn't sell it, so at some point they preferred to take it off the market. Psychology plays some part in this. Not unlike "dark matter" in the Universe, shadow property is "not there" as far as the market is concerned, and yet, it's *very much there*, and it affects the market cycle. By the very definition of shadow property, it's difficult to track, so the statistics may vary depending on whom you ask. But suffice it to say that there were moments in recent Manhattan real estate history when the shadow inventory outweighed the official inventory by well over 200%!

The influence of market cycles on the liquidity of properties depends on that property's price and luxury level. This is something that could be thought of as "market cycle segmentation": not all properties are affected equally.

Here's an important fact to bear in mind: most of the sales in Manhattan real estate occur within the price range between $1 and $2 million. Most of the roughly 10,000 properties sold in Manhattan per year are guaranteed to fall somewhere along that "bell curve". Today these are considered to be moderately priced apartments and the demand remains strong, both in high and low markets.

Everything at $5 million and higher is harder to sell in any market, and becomes incrementally more difficult to sell during a buyers' market. Today we have an estimated 17 months' supply of luxury residential properties for sale in Manhattan.

Besides sales properties, the market also depends on the rental inventory to a large degree. As you remember, real estate is created by banks. Today we see all this massive-scale residential construction going on in Manhattan, which means that the inventory is continuously increasing. But what happens when there's so much of it that the market slows down and the banks end up with a lot of properties they can't sell? Well, when sellers are banks, and developers are waiting for banks to cash out, no one is really desperate. So, if the properties didn't sell, there's always a Plan B.

One solution is to drop the prices. A more profitable alternative may be to convert condominiums into rental apartments. That's exactly what banks do when the market becomes oversaturated. We saw this between from 2009 and 2012 - many buildings developed as condos became rentals, but then "the tide turned", the market moved in the direction of sales, and some rentals became condominiums again.

Changes in urban infrastructure also play a prominent part in the market cycle. The new subway lines under Second Avenue and Eleventh Avenue are contributing to an increased demand for real estate properties in the adjacent neighborhoods. This sways the market toward the "sellers" end. But there are subtle nuances here as well because the availability of new transportation also results in an increase in new developments and conversions in the same neighborhoods. After a certain period of time this saturates the market and sways it toward the "buyers" end. You have to have an excellent sense of timing and develop a sort of "market intuition" to read these changes accurately. This is gained only from experience, and that's why every investor needs a team.

In addition to inventory-based market fluctuations and infrastructure, you should also consider the social aspect of market behavior. Even though it is perhaps not as immediately obvious as it is in places like the stock market or the fashion industry, the "herd mentality" exists in real estate as well, and it can often be observed on the local level in a specific neighborhood or even on a single city block. If someone sold high in a certain neighborhood, all nearby properties will experience a price spike because the sellers will see higher economic potential in the area. This can sometimes escalate into a veritable chain reaction that can make prices in the neighborhood skyrocket.

The market, however, doesn't always support these kinds of "accidental neighborhood price bumps". In fact, bank appraisers or others in real estate financing look at sales trends over the previous 6-12 months before making decisions. Often a bank wouldn't accept as "credible evidence" anything that had been sold outside of that period. Appraisers tend to be pretty good at listening to the market, and in return the market listens to them. The moral of this story: love your friendly neighborhood bank appraiser!

To understand the market situation at a particular time and place, you can do what appraisers do and simply study sales data. This may sound daunting but it's actually very easy today, and it's necessary if you're serious about making maximum profit and want to avoid costly mistakes. You should always track sales—what is being sold and how—in your market of interest.

Remember how in the previous chapter I promised to tell you more about accessing high-quality information? Here's this golden nugget of knowledge for you.

Web platforms like *PropertyShark*, *ACRIS,* and *Corelogic* track the real estate market. Today all this information is public, and this helps investors understand and use market developments to their advantage. Every real estate deal is registered so you can get updates on where and what had been sold and at what price, practically in real time.

I wholeheartedly recommend that you sign up for one or several of such services so you can develop good market awareness. And you should also keep your hand on the pulse of the market in any other possible way. Study the listings. Read *Real Deal* and *Curbed*. Use Google! And pay attention to what's being whispered - you may discover a valuable gold nugget amidst the less glamorous material of real estate rumors. A deal may not even be in the contract phase before it starts affecting trends in your local market. Word-of-mouth is a powerful force in the "small village" of Manhattan real estate, where everybody knows everybody else—or at least claims to!

Ultimately, it's the title closing that represents your most direct touchpoint with the market. It's through closed deals that the market goes up and down, and when you know what deals were closed recently, it's like having real estate GPS: you always know where you are.

Cycles are sometimes smooth, but they can also go through drastic changes. Throughout my career in real estate I've lived through at least four recognizable market cycles and found ways to prosper in most of these. Today, I allow myself to enjoy and make the most of the booming market, but I don't panic when it goes through temporary inactivity. I've learned to wait it out and not lose my patience.

Why sell during a buyer's market? Why buy during a sellers' market?

In a perfect world, buyers would always want to buy in the "top market" (when <u>maximum</u> inventory is available, and therefore the prices are the lowest), and sellers would want to sell in the "low market", aka "bottom market", when the inventory is at the minimum, and therefore the prices are highest.

So, of course, it's reasonable to ask: why would any seller in their right mind want to sell their property during a buyers' market, knowing they won't get the best price? And why would any buyer decide to buy real estate during a sellers' market, knowing they would be paying a much higher price for it? The truth is, all real estate sales and purchases occur because of the strong need to sell or buy. And that's where market cycle becomes secondary and the need to take action becomes the main driving factor.

Sometimes a property becomes available due to a major or dramatic event. An owner or a co-owner dies and their heir does not have the time or inclination to manage the property; children grow up and move out and their parents retire and move to another state; a separation or a divorce dictates the need to liquidate commonly owned properties. Or people may want to sell a property because their 27-year period of property depreciation is about to come to the end; or because their business isn't doing too well in the current market and they need cash to keep it afloat - and so on.

In fact, we observe the "listing non-seller" phenomenon fairly often in real estate: someone lists their property just to test the market and see if they can get a good price for it, but without any true intent to sell. That's not a real seller. Be aware of this! You may fall in love with a property, and never even have a chance to own it because the sale intent just wasn't there in the first place. In real estate investment as with everything else in life, it's always best to try not to develop emotional attachments to material things.

Just as it is with selling, necessity is what ultimately drives real estate purchase. It's often important for me to buy a certain piece of property for a specific reason: maybe it's simply because I need to include it into my portfolio for future development because it would add some unique value to it. Usually in such scenarios you'd most likely be the potential buyer for the property. If your seller knows that, they'll make you pay a much higher price. In fact, if you find yourself in that situation, it really doesn't matter which phase of the market you're in. It could be the ultimate buyers' market and you'd still pay top dollar for that one property, because your urge to buy will drive the price of that property up, and create a local market exception or "pocket" just for your seller.

This brings us to the most important ideas that I'd like to share with you in this book. **In real estate, no one ever buys or sells at the best price.**

That's why whenever a prospective investor asks me: "Should I wait for the prices to fall before I commit to buying a piece of property?" My answer is: "Don't wait. Buy today what you can afford to buy. Use your real estate investment to grow your wealth, and when the market improves, buy more."

Property value and property valuation are always at the core of an eternal argument. The buyer will always feel the property is too expensive, and the seller will always feel it's too cheap. This is the distilled essence of the real estate investment game. If you understand this principle of imperfection and know how to use it, and if you develop the intuitive ability to control and manage this fundamental conflict between a buyer and a seller, you will succeed - both as a buyer, and as a seller!

The balance between your flexibility and your ability to make a firm demand, your ability to distinguish between the need to compromise and the need to draw a line - the proverbial "art of the deal" - is what will define the measure of your success.

A deal is a meeting of the minds. That's why my profession exists: I help buyers and sellers find happy common ground. How do you know if a real estate broker is any good? Here's how: after the deal is closed, both parties - a buyer and a seller - experience the exhilarating sense of victory.

It's not easy to reach this level in my profession. But I'm proud to say that after decades of putting together deals, I am used to seeing both the buyer and seller excited; and they often even become friends - no kidding!! I've directed closings during which entire families of sellers and buyers were present, and I saw these families bond and remain friends for years afterwards. That's because both parties felt certain that they were the ones who won and gained maximum advantage in the deal.

Are you beginning to see how all pieces of this beautiful puzzle fit together? Market cycles, prices, the timing of the sale or purchase, property types and location, your goals, your methodology, your ability to wield data, your own skillset and that of your team - it's all interconnected. Your deep understanding of market cycles and the ability to take advantage of each of its phases can serve as a solid base from which you can assemble everything else.

So, to conclude this chapter why don't we take a look together at some of the ups and downs that happened over the last couple of decades?

The Mid-1990s

The 1990s felt like a magical time to me, probably because I was young and wide-eyed and just getting my first taste of what's possible when you learn your craft. When I look back at that time, I realize it was a rather quaint period. In fact, the mid-1990s was characterized by a slow market. There were very few deals.

There were also fewer real estate brokers. Today there are approximately 20,000 real estate brokers operating in Manhattan, but back then there were a couple of thousand at most. It's a huge industry today, with such behemoths as Douglas Elliman, Corcoran, Brown Harris Stevens and the new cool kid on the block, Compass. All of these people are consummate professionals who know real estate in and out and sell several billions of dollars' worth of properties every year.

The mid-1990s were small-scale by comparison. The $50 - $70 million residential records, set twenty years later by Russian, Chinese, and Arab billionaires were unheard of.

In our wildest imagination, we couldn't foresee The Plaza converted into condominiums or the Mayflower Hotel razed and the gorgeous 15 Central Park West built in its place. We had a limited number of properties to play the real estate game with, and a limited idea of what was possible. No one thought of extreme luxury as the defining factor for the next generation of properties. A building developed on a $50 million budget would have seemed almost improbably luxurious.

Today we see developments that cost $500 million to $3 billion and find them normal. The $4- billion-dollar budget for Central Park Tower would have covered the cost of construction of every condominium in the entire city in the 1990's. Today it's the price for just one building.

Turn of the Millennium

The mid-1990s slump didn't last. A wonderful thing happened to Manhattan real estate: the growth of the American economy due to President Clinton's intelligent presidency and the sudden blossoming of publicly accessible high technology and innovation led to economic growth. Google became a household name, mobile use grew exponentially, and consumer spending reached unprecedented heights. The real estate market in New York immediately reacted with a massive boom.

Starting around 1998 and one through the turn of the millennium, optimism prevailed in the Manhattan real estate community. Real estate prices grew and the investors' appetite for New York City real estate continued to be insatiable. Growth showed every sign of being unstoppable and unlimited. Only a disaster could change this.

And then a true disaster did happen: the September 11, 2001 terror attack.

This act of evil was not only a strike on the World Trade Center, the Pentagon, and the American nation's morale. It was a deliberate attack on the Western economy. And it did what it was intended to do: the catastrophe stopped the economy cold. A lot of people lost their jobs. The Manhattan real estate market was affected on many levels and for many reasons, and the fact that the terrorists specifically targeted and destroyed the Twin Towers, New York City's tallest, most iconic real estate property, was just one of them.

The effect turned out to be long-term. The stock market crashed. Considering that at least 30% of New York City's real estate market is powered by people working in the financial industry, the crash delivered a mortal blow to our industry. After the attack, there were no real estate sales in Manhattan in 2001 and most of 2002. It was few enough to make us to feel that real estate had been knocked dead. Not just in Manhattan - but everywhere.

2002-2008

Then in 2002, to give an "emergency resuscitation" to real estate market nationwide, President George Bush formulated a plan to make mortgages more accessible. Banks supported the initiative and "over-delivered" by making it absurdly easy for almost anyone to receive a mortgage.

To qualify for a mortgage of any size and on great conditions, a person didn't even have to prove their income. They basically just needed to have a pulse and the ability to sign their name. At first, this strategy seemed to work. As if by magic the market was suddenly flooded with inventory. For example, in Battery Park City - the neighborhood that was shut down for half a year due to the World Trade Center recovery efforts - real estate owners who held on to their properties in 2001 and 2002 suddenly wanted to sell.

During the period between 2002 and 2008, we thought we lived in a residential Golden Age. Anybody could buy a house or a condominium with a minimum down-payment. This was a sellers' market: owners of properties for sale could set top prices, and buyers would pay because they had access to seemingly bottomless money wells supplied by the banks. Practically 90% of real estate deals were made possible by financing.

The market crested in 2007-2008. At the top of the market in early 2008, inventory reached historically unprecedented heights, with 12,000 condos available for sale in Manhattan! That number included both new developments and resale.

Unfortunately, this was followed by a major "correction": a true market crisis.

2008-2009

This period was marked by a great deal of drama, suspense, and existential angst. The Wall Street collapse of September 16, 2008 was followed by the news of the Lehman Brothers bankruptcy and the worst Dow Jones fall in history; the end of the Bush era and the political uncertainty of Obama vs McCain; the highest loss of consumer confidence, leading to frugality, especially across the entire luxury market; a shift of mayoralty in NYC from Bloomberg to DiBlasio. All of that took the wind out of the sails of New York's real estate market.

Bliss turned to agony. Real estate prices plummeted by 30 to 40%. Overnight it became a buyers' market, except it was not just any buyers' market but a *cash* buyers' market: some banks collapsed, others were eaten by their larger, toothier competitors, and getting a mortgage became more difficult than ever before. Sellers instantly "clammed up."

Few deals happened in 2008 and 2009, and those that did were "distress deals"; only people under threat of foreclosure sold their properties during that period. The American economy plunged into recession, dragging the world economy down with it. If we look at things from a long-term perspective, we'll see that this was the delayed aftershock of the September 11, 2001, terror attack: the "easy mortgage" solution to the post-attack economy took several years to backfire, but backfire it did.

Even today, nearly two decades after the catastrophe and a decade after the mortgage-induced recession, we see that trust in mortgages has not fully returned, and at least 50% of real estate deals in Manhattan are done with hard cash. That's not necessarily a bad thing, because we're now more or less certain that a credit collapse in real estate won't happen again.

Yes, the market didn't forget the crisis—because it was unforgettable! By 2009, real estate sales in Manhattan just stopped - and it took about 5-6 years for the inventory to decrease completely.

2009-2011

These two years represented the period of stasis in real estate market, the likes of which I've never seen and hope to never see again. They felt like eternity – and nothing was happening during that time, so there's nothing to write about!

2011-2015

But even the worst devastation never lasts forever. By the end of 2011 the shock began to subside. Life moved on, people regained the need to sell and buy properties; banks loosened their restrictions and started offering mortgages again. Miraculously, the market picked up, started gaining momentum – and by 2015 the activities were in full swing. In fact, 2015 was one of the most remarkable year in Manhattan real estate, with median condo prices reaching $1.5 million, median price per square foot setting the new record at $1,645 – and despite that growth in cost, the average time on the market fell to the record low of 73 days (which means that some properties were purchased weeks or even days after they were listed). The inventory and sales of new developments skyrocketed, despite the jump in prices to median $2.4 million!

2015 - Present

In 2015, there were approximately 2,500 condos for sale. The market "bottomed out" and inventory started climbing up again. In 2016 and 2017 the market stabilized: more residences were built, and today we have approximately 9,000 condos and co-ops available for sale. Historically this is the second highest inventory after 2008's all-time record.

Between 2011 and 2015, it was a sellers' market - the demand was a lot higher than the supply. Now as I sit here writing this, the market is in transition. Until only a couple of months ago real estate prices in Manhattan were at their highest, and near the 7th year of the cycle. That felt a bit too long - and sure enough: in 2018 prices started dropping and we've now entered a buyers' market again. Due to an abundance of inventory and a new factor—the huge amount of data available today to everyone publicly—this buyer's market promises to empower buyers like no market in real estate history.

Buyers have never had so many opportunities and tools at their disposal. They can now show the seller they have an edge and the ability to negotiate the price as they wish. We don't know how long this will last—two, three, or five years - but we do know that the next seller's market will come, and we can expect the prices to reach even greater heights then.

Real estate is a tangible, physical thing, which in a way makes it more important than money because it's more "real." Even though cash is king, buying property gives you something you can point to and say: "This is mine. I know exactly what that's worth right now. I have a pretty good idea of what it can be worth in the future, not only because I know how to invest well, but because everyone on my team knows what they're doing, and they confirmed my faith in this property."

That brings us to our next subject.

Chapter VIII: The Investor's Team

The truth is, as much as you might want to, you can't just see a property you like, snap your fingers, and have someone hand you the keys. You need a team of trusted people to work with you - to negotiate, navigate, and close the deal. It's largely the work that team does together that informs the success of the deal. Before any deal is closed, there must be negotiations, forms, payments, financing, legal issues, and much more. The people on your side in the trenches while you wage that battle are all-important.

Let's take a look at the team members who can help make that happen and what pitfalls exist in what they do.

The Lawyer

In New York investors are always represented by a real estate attorney on any transaction. At the risk of saying the obvious, you should remember that the lawyer who works with you on your real estate deal should be an expert in real estate law. As a real estate investor, you certainly don't want to be represented by a personal injury lawyer. When in doubt, ask your broker for a reference. Chances are they've worked with at least one or two they trust implicitly.

Over the course of the entire transaction, your lawyer will protect you and make sure you're getting full value. Your lawyer will also verify that there are no mistakes or discrepancies anywhere. Always inform your lawyer about all the details and nuances of the deal. That includes the price of purchase, how quickly you plan on closing the deal, what kind of down payment you're responsible for, issues in the environmental report, as well as any general concerns that you might have about the property.

When purchasing a property, it's extremely important to make sure there are no real estate taxes owed on that property, no previously accrued debt, and that the seller has closed their mortgage. Your lawyer will make sure that all of that is as it should be. The lawyer works directly with the Title Company, bank, environmental regulators, and land surveyor to make sure every aspect of the transaction is transparent and clean.

Lawyers also check the FHA statements directly with the bank to confirm the correctness of payments. This way they can ensure that the deal is closed and that all payments to the bank are calculated correctly.

Some of the things that may raise the red flags with an expert lawyer may be small "tells" that the building, while maintaining a successful "public persona" (and corresponding prices), may be in some kind of trouble. Sometimes these signs are more obvious. For example, if a building has very low reserve funds, that's almost like having a huge sign in front of it that says "bankrupt". You shouldn't rush to conclusions because some of the building management companies responsible for higher-end buildings may have perfectly legitimate but aggressive "spending styles," so other factors in the financial statement should also be carefully considered. On the other hand, such a small thing as monthly charges that haven't gone up for years may sound like a good thing—but it most certainly isn't. To a skilled lawyer this would signify that the building is probably being mismanaged.

Furthermore, the final piece in the real estate transaction—the signing of the contract and money exchange—is overseen by lawyers on the buyer and seller sides of the deal. Money is moved between parties through the lawyers' escrow accounts— also known as IOLA, an acronym that stands for "Interest on Lawyer Account". The lawyers deliver the funds to one another, and then they are disbursed to the seller. That is the only way your transaction can conclude in New York State. Consider it one less thing you have to worry about.

A lawyer's work in a real estate investment transaction usually takes between 30 to 60 days on average. Depending on the complexity of the deal, their cost could end up being anywhere between $2,500 and $5,000. I always recommend that you agree to a fixed fee deal with a lawyer, as there could be many unpredictable variants that arise throughout the process. In case the lawyer's work volume increases, you don't want to be stuck paying by the hour. If you did decide to go that route, you could try to set a cap on lawyer fees and they'll know not to exceed an agreed-upon sum.

I should note that in some states, hiring a lawyer for real estate transactions is not obligatory. For example, in the state of Florida—where I am also licensed—the broker handles the entire process and a lawyer is not required. Here the broker, with the help of the title company, fully calculates and aligns the balance of the payment, aligns debit with credit, and delivers the closing statement.

The Mortgage Broker & Bank

The success of your purchase often depends on your leverage. I'm not referring to the pressure that you can exert on the seller, but rather to the fact that a bank's financing is literally referred to as "leverage" in a real estate purchase here.

You should have already be pre-qualified for a mortgage with a brokerage before pursuing a property purchase. Your real estate broker should have plenty of good connections for a good mortgage broker. I know I can rattle off quite a few great bankers I routinely send clients to that provide excellent, satisfying service.

It's important during any real estate transaction to make sure that the conditions of your financing are in good standing. Specifically, you want to make sure you get a low percentage rate for the length of your mortgage, whether it is 1.5 years, five years, or 30 years. You also want to make sure that your closing costs are as low as possible. These are all things a good mortgage broker will help you with.

Most importantly, you want to make sure that you are not personally guaranteeing a purchase when it comes to real estate. I mentioned earlier that the real estate market can change quickly, and your decisions may change as well. You may want to hold onto your property longer than expected. Whatever the case, you'll want to ensure that your personal properties are not being held as collateral, dependent on the success or failure of this purchase.

There are some banks that will agree to finance you with a non-recourse loan. So, in theory, if you default on the loan, the bank can seize the property in question but not your personal assets. However, these kinds of loans often require a larger down payment. This can be as much as 25, 30, or even 35 percent - and that's for a prime residence.

Personally, I always recommend that an investor sign an agreement that contains a clause stating that the investor is not making a personal guarantee on the investment. When it comes to rental agreements, especially for commercial properties, I will even agree to sign a "good guy clause." This kind of agreement allows for any renters or tenants in the property to be released from liability if a rental agreement is terminated early, assuming that they vacate the rental space on time and leave it in a favorable condition. So, if your company is going through a rough period and needs to vacate your apartment, you simply leave the place in pristine condition, take the key to the bank, and are not held personally responsible.

The Title Company

Apologies to the other members on your team, but the title company is really the cornerstone of any real estate deal! The title company that is in charge of checking and confirming that the piece of real estate you're about to purchase is exactly what the seller claims it to be. Once that is confirmed, they will issue title insurance, which will come in handy if there ends up being any type of issue with the title. It also protects you and the bank from any legal claims or lawsuits that could ever arise over the title.

Seek out recommendations for a good title company but definitely lean on your real estate broker for suggestions. Just like with lawyers and mortgage brokers, I keep a handy list of title companies I know I can trust to take good care of my clients. Any good broker should be doing the same.

When you buy something - anything, really- you must know that you're making a rock-solid purchase. This becomes vital when you're making a purchase that costs millions of dollars. If you make a well-informed decision, that purchase becomes the foundation of your financial success as an investor.

The cost of title examination and insurance will be included in your closing costs, which are approximately three percent of the purchase price without financing. If you work with the bank, that will bring closing costs up to around five percent because of mortgage tax, which stands at two percent in New York State. If you're buying a luxury condo or property, you should also consider the so-called "mansion tax". Until very recently this tax was very straightforward: one percent on any home sold for upwards of $1 million. But starting on July 1, 2019, the buyers of properties priced over $1,999,999 will face higher mansion taxes, ranging from 1.25% to 3.9% (the largest figure applied to properties bought for $25 million and higher).

Including miscellaneous fees, your closing costs should come to between three-to-ten percent of the purchase price.

I want to tell you a story that illustrates the importance of a title company's role in a real estate investor's life. I was selling a garage building to one of my clients. It was really important for the buyer that everything absolutely fit according to city standards and that he didn't accrue any additional risks if his property happened to develop any issues.

This was a huge garage in a very good neighborhood located on a multimillion-dollar property, and it also happened to be his first real estate investment. He ordered the environmental report and discovered much to his and our surprise, that his garage shared a load-bearing wall with the adjacent garage. The seller, of course, omitted this detail. The problem? If two buildings share one wall, who owns the wall?

Upon first hearing about the shared wall, my client refused to buy the garage building. He started asking all the important questions. Who is responsible if the wall cracks or if anything happens to it? How do we handle maintenance? What if we want to raze the garage and build a new property? We reached out to our title company for answers. Fortunately, a trusted title expert and his team explained to us that when row homes, or in this case garages for row homes, are attached, it's very common to see multiple properties share load-bearing walls. They might even see two different builders end up sharing a wall during construction. It's also common for the two properties to have once belonged to a single owner.

Once my client's concerns had been addressed and his questions answered, he agreed to buy the building. And since the seller didn't mention the wall during the negotiation and just sent the contract directly to our lawyer, we requested a perfectly justified discount of several thousand dollars-more than enough to cover the environmental report, land survey, and title insurance.

The Appraiser

Another part of the real estate buying process in New York is the appraisal. You can hire your own appraiser to find out the value of the property you are purchasing, but I wouldn't recommend that. Usually the bank will expect to have their own appraisal and will not make their decision based on the results of an outside appraiser, so it would end up being a waste of money. The bank will tell you which appraiser they want you to use. You'll have to pay for this service, but at least you know the bank will accept that appraisal.

On average, the appraisal of an apartment may cost you around $1,000, while a commercial appraisal will run you closer to $3,000, but these are ballpark numbers. I've seen apartments with appraisal costs in the low hundreds and I've seen luxury units go well above $1,000. A good broker will know how to set your expectations beforehand.

The Surveyor

One of the most overlooked aspects of buying property in New York City is the land survey. It's actually important to do this because it shows you the real size of the land you're going to purchase. There may be existing maps or records of the land size, but a surveyor can come in and re-measure the property in order to give you updated values. It's entirely possible that the assessment of the size of the land will change, based on improved scientific methods or new data.

As a rule, I recommend taking the extra step and doing a "land survey with elevation," even if it costs you a little more than a regular land survey. If you're knocking something down or renovating, your contractor will appreciate it all the more since it will include extra information, including city easements such as drains or Con Edison wire placements. It'll also cut down on the need for additional surveys, as well as charges from an architect who might need to adjust plans down the road.

Partners

If you're looking to buy a condo, co-op, or a house to live in, you're probably not going to do so with a financial partner. But just in case you're considering a commercial property or building investment, or if you want to invest in one or more residential units to be used as a source of passive income, you'll want to consider the importance of a partner in your deal-making strategy and plan. I call this kind of partnership "a marriage" because the success of the deal often depends on the relationship between you and your partner.

There are all different kinds of partnerships. Your partner might be an absentee owner, someone who gives you the capital for the deal but who otherwise remains out of the negotiations because they trust you to deliver a return on their investment. You can have a working partner who works side-by-side with you on all matters concerning the deal and has input just as you do. Whatever the structure, I insist that you should always discuss it beforehand. You want to make sure that all your partners have signed a management agreement that clarifies everyone's roles, ability to provide input, expectations, and obligations.

It's also important that you form a corporation for each and every purchase you and your partners make. Whether that is an LLC (limited liability company) or LLP (limited liability partnership), you'll want to get that squared away early. This allows you the possibility to avoid personal responsibility for any property should anything go wrong. It will also help you save on any potential court fees or expenses.

When it comes to decision-making, setting expectations early is critical. Everyday business decisions, such as the day-to-day operations, should be done by the general manager, who is responsible for participating in all aspects of the deal. Think of this person as the captain of the ship. Smaller everyday issues should ultimately fall to one person, i.e., the working partner. However, when it comes to the major decisions that make or break the deal (buying, selling, refinancing, etc.), these should always be done together among the partners and management team.

As a rule, partners have certain expectations. You and your partner must be always transparent and sincere with one another—hence the marriage analogy. Never make assumptions and always break down every aspect of the deal. Only when all the partners are on the same page should you move forward. The real estate business can be tricky and unpredictable. You have to think in the long term, much like with the stock market. Sometimes a deal that looked like a sure thing falls through or gets delayed, and you don't want your partner blaming you because you promised something you couldn't deliver.

In America there's something called Tenancy in Common (TIC) that applies to any real estate deal where two or more people are partners. Simply put TIC is how the ownership of a property is represented between multiple owners. In this instance, "tenants" doesn't refer to the people in the apartment or the house but rather the people who own it. It's just one of a few ownership or investment structures—along with sole owner-ship, joint tenancy, and "tenancy in the entirety". There are a lot of benefits to TIC ownership but you want to make sure that you are clear on what it means, what risks are involved, what advantages it gives you, and how it prevents or causes any issues from cropping up.

A TIC ownership can be between as few as two and as many as 30 investors on a property. These owners do not need to establish any kind of relationship outside of the partnership, though they can also be married or related. The ownership stakes don't have to be even, either. One partner can control 50 percent of the property, while the two other partners each control 25 percent. And upon the death of a co-tenant in a TIC ownership, that share automatically passes on to his/her heirs, so your estate wouldn't lose control of a property or the revenue it generates in the event of your death.

As a TIC owner, you're probably not going to be crawling around on the roof fixing loose shingles. It usually means you're the kind of property owner who enjoys the income and tax benefits of a property without getting your hands dirty all the time and employs on-site management.

Remember Your Due Diligence!

Like most people, I assume you don't enjoy being preached to, especially by real estate brokers like me who like to repeat themselves, but this subject is so important that I'm going straight up to the pulpit. As a rule, remember that every piece of property comes with its own unique concerns. Whether it's a house, apartment, or commercial building, each one brings different issues and questions with it.

If you're buying a commercial property, are there current tenants? If so, how long do their leases last? Can you change the leases when you become the owner of the building or unit? You'll have to check to make sure everything in the current rental contract fits the promises made by the seller.

And, of course, you have to double check in order to make sure everything the seller told you about the property is true—it usually won't be! This is critical because New York State dictates that real estate purchases are "arm's length transactions". This means that buyers and sellers enter into these transactions independently and not required to look out for each other's best interests in the sale. It's meant to ensure no collusion exists between buyer and seller, but it also means both parties are acting in their own self-interest.

For example, upon purchasing a building full of renting tenants, each tenant will be asked to sign something called estoppel certificate, which says that each tenant agrees to the condition of the lease and accepts the truth of the lease shown to you by the seller. We once had a situation where the rent numbers that the seller gave us were actually lower than the reality. However, due to some mysterious law of physics I had been unable to pinpoint, it often turns out to be the other way around. The good news is that discovering this during the negotiation provides you with the opportunity to negotiate your price down based on expected rent revenue.

The nuances you discover during due diligence are extremely important and can go a long way towards saving you money. Each team member comes at the negotiation and details from a different angle and can identify potential issues or concerns like the previous one in order to save you money or save you from investing in a bad property. It could be the discovery of real rent, an easement the seller didn't mention or know about, or a discovery about land rights. Either way you need every member of your team to be an expert.

I once had a situation where we wanted to install new windows in a building only to find out that window rights had been sold! Not only that, but the building had no right to include windows on a certain side thanks to a previously unknown easement. Now I know to always check for these kinds of things: you simply never know who knows what they know or don't know!

The Real Estate Broker

We've talked a lot about the team that an investor needs to assemble in order to buy property in New York City. The real estate broker occupies a central, special place on that team. That's why I chose to be a broker: so I could deliver maximum value to my clients.

You want to look for a broker with experience in the kind of deal that you are looking to make. You don't just want a broker who has made one or two of these deals, but hundreds of them. This gives them the ability to give you solid advice during every stage of the deal. An intelligent real estate investor values the importance of good advice and expertise. If you have to pay a slightly higher broker's commission for this, trust me: its money well spent.

But what is it exactly that you're paying your broker *for*? The answer is: you're paying a broker so that they can save you a lot more money than what you paid them. The broker's commission really is a solid investment!

Throughout the book I mentioned a few situations where having a real estate broker may save you, an investor, from losing money or, in some cases, from a great deal of moral suffering. Let me provide a few more.

If you're looking for a place in a new city or in an unfamiliar neighborhood, you'll be prone to errors of judgement. It's the broker's responsibility to save you and your family from being stuck for the next half a decade in an area where the nearest decent school is a mile and a half away, the crime rate is highest in the entire city, or from a building with a troubled financial situation as well as major engineering issues.

If you've never bought real property before, I guarantee that you will find the process overwhelming; being overwhelmed, it's easy to overlook a seemingly small but crucial detail. Once that something is neglected, something else will be disregarded, and as a result you may experience a chain reaction that costs you time, money, nerves, and often the actual property that you were so eager to buy slips right through your fingers. Buying property for the first time? Do yourself a huge favor and hire experienced realtor to watch your back.

If you work crazy hours, you should delegate your real estate search to a professional. You, of all people, understand the importance of delegation and separation of duties.

Most importantly if you're buying property not as your prime residence but as an investment and source of passive income, you will benefit the most from the broker's ability to formulate effective short-term and long-term investment strategies - something that comes into play with every real estate purchase, but becomes especially important if your main goal for real estate purchases is wealth building.

So, how does this work? As I mentioned, both the buyer and seller are only obligated to serve their own self-interests. But the broker's loyalty is to their client. In my twenty-plus years in real estate, I have never encountered a situation where a property was exactly as it had been described by the seller. Some of the differences were very small, while others were massive.

Why is that so? When a seller knows there's something that may result in a noticeable decrease in price, they can't be expected to volunteer that information. Often enough though, the seller isn't an expert and doesn't have any intent to cheat anyone: they simply don't know something, or maybe have no idea where to even look. Similarly, I don't think many of the buyers have this expertise either. So, while you always need to do your own preliminary due diligence, have a broker who leaves no stone unturned.

The work of a broker is somewhat similar to that of a private eye. It has to be thorough and painstaking. Its ultimate objective is simple: to find out the truth. I go into every deal with positive expectations and an open mind, but I also do all of my investigations thoroughly and never make assumptions. The seller might be honest, but that doesn't mean everything they say is correct.

Here's an example. Buildings in New York City are often built wall-to-wall and they sometimes come with easements. An easement is the right by one party to enter or access a property that they don't actually own. Sometimes the previous owner or seller will not mention that there is an easement involved. Sometimes they might not even be aware of one themselves, as easements can sometimes go back decades or even centuries.

That's exactly what happened in one deal I did where, upon investigation, we found a handwritten easement note from 1961 signed by former buyers and sellers. The easement said that a door on the first floor of an adjacent building was obligatory so that the tenants of that building could enter or exit easily. However, the only way to create that door was through the neighboring building on the other side of the shared wall. Over time, that door and pathway had been closed off and forgotten about. Fast-forward to our purchase of the neighboring building, which we had plans to raze.

If the buyer acted without a broker, even if they had discovered the easement before the deal closed, this would inevitably have resulted in extra tension between buyer and seller, and might have ruined the entire deal. More likely though, the buyer would be blissfully unaware of the easement, and would've discovered the door after knocking down a wall, at which point they would have had the shock of a lifetime, because this would mean making a major adjustment to the architectural plan, creating a special corridor for that door, and incurring massive extra costs.

Luckily, we did our due diligence and clearly explained to the seller the array of problems the easement would create for the buyer down the road - and lowered our offer on the property. Although the seller didn't even realize the easement existed, the argument we presented was iron clad. We were able to persuade them to see things from our point of view, and they wisely accepted the offer. This became a win-win scenario: the seller successfully sold the property for the largest reasonable amount to be expected, and the buyer acquired the property for less than originally expected—and the price difference was enough to cover both the broker's fee and the cost of handling the easement issue.

This wasn't blind luck, but a result of thorough research and hard work—which makes it a pleasure for me to be a broker! One very good reason to consider hiring a good broker is the simple fact that bidding wars are extremely likely when it comes to commercial property in Manhattan. It's up to the seller's broker to get the highest offer and go with the buyer who is most likely to close the deal, keep their word, and commit to all of the promises made during every step of the negotiation.

Sellers like to say that "buyers are liars" who often don't follow through on the obligations they agreed to at first. The truth is that buyers want to make sure that they get the best value possible for their money. When you make an offer in Manhattan, especially in a seller's market, it's entirely possible you'll be one of thirty or even forty offers if it's a hot property deal or in a great neighborhood. All of them are interested, have money, and want to get the deal done. So how does the seller choose? The seller simply wants to get the highest price from the best buyer.

That's when having a broker who knows how to handle complex negotiating scenarios comes in handy. A broker works with the client and the opposing party to make sure that the very best deal happens. A really good broker finds a way to organize a deal in such a way that both sides - buyer and seller - are happy!

There are several "rounds" in any bidding war. The first round establishes the structure and order according to which the sale or purchase will be made. The system for making the next round of bids is then created and those offers are made, usually as closed bids. When the deadline is reached, all interested parties should have their final and highest offers in.

Even when you break it down to highest offers, you're often still left with at least two buyers. From here the buyer and broker should be going directly to the seller, speaking openly about the procedure and details. The last round of bidding pits the remaining buyers against one another until the winner is chosen. The second-place bidder should stick around, however, just in case the winning bidder defaults or decides to walk away from the deal in the end.

I have just one more story to make my point regarding the value of a good broker. When you buy any piece of property, there's always a certain risk. That risk may be justified or it may not. There are a lot of factors that can influence your investment. Brothers Arthur and William Zekendorf bought the Mayflower Hotel in 2004. This great location attracted many developers, buyers, and investors over the years, but it was the Zekendorf brothers who "snatched it up", along with a few adjacent lots, for just over $400 million. Situated on Central Park West between 61st and 62nd streets, the building didn't have much historic value and wasn't a landmark… which meant that it was a terrific redevelopment opportunity, rather than renovation material. The brothers checked and the costs of renovating the hotel were not warranted.

So, they razed the hotel in 2006 and put plans into place to replace the site and the surrounding lots with two towers at 15 Central Park West. The plan was to fill the buildings with luxury condominiums. Now, there weren't many developments like this at the time on the Upper West Side and many people felt that the market wouldn't support the new housing. Still, they pushed forward and constructed the buildings anyway.

Many of my clients didn't want to risk buying anything in these buildings, but a few of them did. One of the apartments that I sold, a 28th-floor unit in the taller building, wasn't given a guarantee of a park view. In fact, my clients didn't even get to see a floor plan. They had to rely on the assumption that architect Robert Stern would live up to his reputation.

Still, my buyer decided to take the risk and purchased that unit for approximately $6 million. Even for a wealthy person, that is a risky proposition. However, with solid support from my team, I reviewed every document and detail related to the project. As a result of my research I felt confident about the purchase, and advised the client to go ahead with the deal. We helped the client to control everything we could, from the financing to the contract details. The purchase was completed in 2006 with plans to move into the apartment in 2008.

2008 arrived and my clients were pleasantly surprised when they entered their new apartment for the first time. The apartment had cleared the lower tower and had an incredible view of Central Park. Not to mention that the place itself was stunning. This apartment is valued today at $20 million. That's not a bad return on that initial investment...

The really satisfying part for me, both professionally and personally, is the trust that I have built up with this client. If I went to them right now with a new property that I believed would be even better, I know that they would trust me enough to come take a look at it. That's because at 15 Central Park West I took care of them every step of the way in the same way that the way loyal Samwise Gamgee took care of Frodo as they traveled all the way to Mordor and back to the Shire in *Lord of the Rings*. (I've been writing this book on-and-off for over a decade, and since the very beginning I hoped I'd find a justification for including a *Lord of the Rings* reference!)

And that's that. Thank you for reading my book!

Yours truly,

Elliot Bogod

Acknowledgements:

This book exists thanks to all the wonderful clients I had the privilege to serve over the last two decades - real estate investors and sellers who asked me deep questions, relied on my answers, and motivated me to be the best professional I can be. Thank you for trusting me with your happiness!

I owe deep gratitude to colleagues and friends who shared this journey with me - real estate brokers, developers, marketers, attorneys, financial and title experts, educators - people who supported me in this decision to share my knowledge with public, in the form of a book. I'm profoundly grateful to REBNY, Miami Realtors Association and Forbes Real Estate Council. It's a great honor to be a member of these organizations!

This book is my way to give back to the industry and my responsibility to payback for wonderful opportunities it presented throughout the years.

I reserve special thanks for Broadway Realty team: Natalia Dolinsky, Alexander Bogod and Dimitri Vorontzov. You guys rock!

And with all my heart I'd like to thank you, my dear reader. Thank you for picking up this book - I hope you found it useful!

About the Author:

Elliot Bogod is a real estate author, educator, blogger and a founder and managing director of Broadway Realty, a major New York real estate brokerage.

In the course of his twenty-plus years in real estate, Elliot has personally sold over $2 billion worth of Manhattan residential and commercial real estate, including residences in such prominent buildings as Time Warner Towers, Trump International Tower, Trump Riverside Boulevard, Fifteen Central Park West, 10 West End Avenue and The Plaza Condominium Residences.

A notable thought leader in the real estate industry, Elliot contributes articles to Forbes, NY Times, Wall Street Journal, NY Real Estate Magazine, Real Estate Weekly and other prominent publications. Elliot's popular luxury real estate blog presents detailed overviews of the most remarkable new and converted buildings, with abundant details and rich, high-quality photographic illustrations.

A member of the Real Estate Board of New York and the Realtor Association of Miami-Dade County, Elliot was among the first in a group of thirty top Manhattan brokers to receive a NYRS (New York Residential Specialist) designation from the Real Estate Board of New York (REBNY). Elliot's professional pedigree is certified by New York Real Estate Institute, Real Estate Division at the Academy of Continuing Education and the Gold Coast Real Estate School.

Elliot Bogod resides in Manhattan with his wife and two children. He is a continuous contributor to multiple nonprofits and a member of Wall Street Synagogue

www.ingramcontent.com/pod-product-compliance
Lightning Source LLC
Chambersburg PA
CBHW051417090426
42737CB00014B/2711